SKY SAILORS

THE STORY OF THE WORLD'S AIRSHIPMEN

CES MOWTHORPE

SUTTON PUBLISHING

First published in 1999 by
Sutton Publishing Limited · Phoenix Mill
Thrupp · Stroud · Gloucestershire · GL5 2BU

British Library Cataloguing in Publication Data
A catalogue record for this book is available from the British Library

ISBN 0-7509-2218-4

 ^{TM} ALAN SUTTON™ and SUTTON™ are the trade marks of Sutton Publishing Limited

Typeset in 11/14pt Garamond.
Typesetting and origination by
Sutton Publishing Limited.
Printed in Great Britain by
Redwood, Trowbridge, Wiltshire.

Dedicated to the late David Cook of Tynemouth, Northumberland, son of Flying Officer George Cook. Cardington Tower Officer and ex-airship Coxswain. At the time of his death, David Cook's knowledge of British airships was unsurpassed.

The engineer of the centre starboard engine-car of R.32 pauses to have his photograph taken by his compatriot in the forward starboard engine-car of R.32 as she flies 1500 ft above the North Sea at about 50 mph. The legs of his fellow engineer of the same engine-car can be seen dangling from the hatchway onto the engine-car walkway. Above the walkway is the cable support, for the assistance of those of a nervous disposition. (*Ces Mowthorpe Collection*)

Contents

Illustrations

Preface

An avid aviation enthusiast, and practising pilot since the age of sixteen, the study of airships has been a major interest of mine for forty years. I was born in the era of R.101 – R.100 was built just 'down the road at Howden' – and my parents frequently retold stories about wartime 'Zepps'. When a 'petrol tank thrown overboard by a Zeppelin damaged by the Atwick gun' fell into Grandfather Stennett's field, being the local wheelwright, he promptly cut it in half and made two feeding troughs for cattle. 'Howden Pigs', Lowthorpe mooring-out station and other stories stimulated in me a great curiosity about this, now bygone, form of flying.

During the late 1940s and '50s, reliable sources of information about airships were few. Because of the huge advances in aeroplane manufactured during the Second World War, airships, as far as Europe was concerned, had become as extinct as the dinosaur and the excellent Zeppelin Museum at Friedrichshafen, Germany, had been wiped out by RAF bombing raids.

In Britain a wealth of information was hidden away, or lost, during the Second World War and research has required seemingly endless time and money. Local records were non-existent because of security measures in force during the First World War. Even known deaths were not recorded in the usual 'civilian' manner. Then, in the early 1960s, I wrote a brief account for *Yorkshire Air News* about a Coastal airship from Howden (C.11) that had hit a hill at Scarborough, in April 1917. This opened a wide door. Mr David Cook from Tynemouth read the article and arranged to visit me. A friendship formed, and through his late father's connection with airships, a considerable amount of material emerged. Knowing I had a serious ambition to write what we called 'a comprehensive book' about British airships, David passed on much valuable information prior to his untimely death.

David Cook's father was Flg Off George Cook, DSM, Tower Officer in charge of the mooring-mast at Cardington, in Bedfordshire. His service had started at Farnborough, with the then Naval Wing of No. 1 Company, Air Battalion. As coxswain he flew in *Beta*, *Delta*, several 'Coastals', Nos 4, 5 and 6 at Howden (as part of the Rigid Trials Crew), No. 9r, No. 23r and finally R.31. It was on the latter that he was responsible, with six volunteers, for securing the upper fin when it collapsed in mid-air. Some days later, while clambering high inside R.31 examining the gas-cells, he was overcome by leaking hydrogen and fell unconscious into the keel, suffering serious injuries.

David's work took him around the country and he utilised this to visit as many of his late father's ex-airship friends as possible. Knowing my wish to write a book (*Battlebags*) he freely allowed me to take notes and copy any of his photographs. His great interest in 'lighter-than-air' craft led him to mount a number of exhibitions of airship photographs around the North of England and to broadcast on local radio.

Another great help was the late Wg Cdr 'Wally' Dunn, OBE, an ex-Halton 'brat'. As a wireless operator, he flew out of Howden on the 'North Seas' during 1920–21. Posted to fly on R.38 to America, he was bitterly disappointed when this was cancelled and he was sent to Gibraltar on flying-boats instead. Listening out from Gibraltar he was 'working' his chum on R.38 when 'transmissions ceased abruptly'. R.38 had broken up in flight over the Humber! During the Second World War, Wg Cdr Dunn was Signals Officer to 617 Squadron (the Dambusters) and the man who handed the famous 'Nigger' message to Barnes Wallis. He freely shared his wealth of knowledge.

Over the last twenty years a number of excellent books about airships have been written (see Bibliography) but they only cover the subject generally. No previous publication until *Battlebags* attempted to identify and describe operations of each single British airship. However, *Battlebags* dealt mainly with the airships themselves. Equally important were the airshipmen who flew and operated these, and all other airships. Early aviation depended greatly upon the skill and daring of its aviators. Present-day reliability and sophistication were unheard of, and every flight was a landmark occasion. Thus a breed of men materialised who for two decades pioneered all that has prospered since. Airshipmen during the first decade of practical aviation outnumbered aeroplane pioneers. Great innovations in aircraft, two world wars and the bad publicity brought about by a small number of horrifying airship disasters changed the picture. Today, the pioneer airshipmen are a forgotten species. It is only proper that before time wipes out all traces, some of their exploits should be placed on the record.

Ces Mowthorpe
Hunmanby
June 1999

Acknowledgements

I would like to pay thanks to the late Mr David Cook, son of the late Sqn Ldr George Cook, DSM, Tower Officer at Cardington, for his assistance with this book, and also to the late Wg Cdr 'Wally' Dunn OBE of Bridlington, East Yorkshire. I have outlined their assistance more fully in the preface to this book. Their contributions made this book possible.

Of equal importance are their 'old pals' who passed on so many valuable contributions which have ended up in these pages. Their names are forever linked with the lighter-than-air pioneers of this country: Beckford-Ball, 'Jerry' Long, Havers, York-Moore and many others. Wg Cdr Dunn's association with Sir Barnes Wallis (from their Dambusters work in 617 Squadron) proved very helpful. Tim Elmhirst, nephew of the late AVM T.W. Elmhirst, was also instrumental, lending me a copy of his late uncle's *Memoirs*. Countless other ex-airshipmen have unwittingly contributed information through their contact with the above people – which has eventually found its way into my records. If any of these, or their relatives, get in touch with me I will be delighted to acknowledge them if further editions are published.

Thanks also go to Mr Naylor of the Royal Aeronautical Society; Mr Graeme Mottram and Mr Richardson of the Fleet Air Arm Museum, Yeovilton; countless members of the Public Record Office at Kew, who have rendered me vital assistance during my visits there; and Nick Forder, one-time compiler of 'Bookshelf' in *Cross & Cockade* – the assistance rendered to me by members of *Cross & Cockade*, the Society of World War One Aero Historians, has been invaluable. I must also thank a kindred spirit, Brian Turpin, whose knowledge of airship development in general and British airships in particular, is among the foremost in Britain today; he spent much time reading my proof and offering corrections and improvements, as well as providing a number of photographs. With regard to *Sky Sailors* and the author's previous publication *Battlebags*, the Airship Heritage Trust staff at Cardington, especially Philip and Margaret Neaverson, went to great lengths to find certain rare photographs. Permission has also been granted by the Airship Heritage Trust journal *Dirigible* and its editor Nick Walmsley for the reproduction of some interesting details from its articles. Thanks also to Tom Jamison, of Hull, for his assistance over the years.

One of the most important contributors has been Stuart Leslie from Scarborough. The photographic collection JMB/GSL and his own tremendous knowledge of the early years of the RNAS/RFC/RAF have been placed at my disposal at all times. Thanks again, Stuart.

Mr Peter London has rendered a valuable service, lending me previously unpublished photographs of RNAS Mullion and its airships.

I am also grateful to the late A.H. Crump for his splendid album and RAF Cranwell for their records.

Introduction

Battlebags, was the result of thirty years of research at the Public Record Office, Imperial War Museum, Fleet Air Arm Museum, RAF Museum, British Library, Royal Aeronautical Society, etc., two visits to the Zeppelin Museum at Friedrichshafen and many interviews with ex-airshipmen. It is a history of every British recorded airship that has flown. That was the reason it was written. While researching the lives and stories of many of the airshipmen that became known to me, it was only natural, with the success of *Battlebags*, that these examples of man's conquest of the air, little known in the 1990s, should be recorded for posterity.

Unlike an aeroplane, airships, especially the huge Zeppelin-type rigids, have a great affinity with sea-going ships, especially sailing ships. Taking them in and out of their sheds, mooring to the mast, are reminiscent of guiding a ship to her harbour berth or dock. Navigating airships over water for sometimes days on end – even in the 1920s, airships did this – was a work of art familiar to their sea-going cousins. Controlling an airship crew, whether three or twenty-three, demanded similar qualities to that of a captain and his ship's crew.

The envelopes of non-rigid airships were attached to their cars or gondolas by masses of cordage both inside and out, in a similar manner to the masts of a sailing-ship. Larger dirigibles had two 'helmsmen' keeping a steady course (hopefully) in both the vertical and directional planes, in a similar manner to an ordinary ship's helmsman.

Clambering about in and on top of an airship flying at 40–50 mph, 1,500 ft above the waves is very reminiscent of sailors working in the rigging of a tall ship, shortening sail in a squall. It seemed a natural progression for airships to be flown by the various navies. Flying over water, without hills or valleys (which cause turbulence at lower altitudes) is perhaps the ideal working space for smaller airships. Royal Naval airshipmen, when returning to base after a long patrol coined the expression 'humped, bumped and b——— about', during the last hour while again flying over land against a strong head wind.

Perhaps most of all, airships were dependent upon the weather. Ninety per cent of shipwrecks are caused by ships running into land. Likewise airships were most vulnerable when close to mother earth. The ability of the large rigid airship to fly around bad weather and if necessary to remain airborne until safe to approach her base,was the secret of the Zeppelin's success in the 1930s.

Arguably the finest airship captain of his day was Dr Eckener. He flew the *Graf Zeppelin* around the globe, to the North Pole, and instituted regular transatlantic flights between 1928 and 1936. As a boy, Dr Eckener had been a keen small-boat sailor, spending all his spare time on the waters of the North Sea. It was this experience, together with a constant study of aerology (now known as meteorology) which ensured the success of these pioneering flights. Only an airship could have made these flights, prior to the Second World War.

Airshipmen were truly sailors of the sky and like sailors everywhere, they had to overcome all obstacles, on their own and often in adverse conditions.

Three excellent photographs taken by
the W/T Operator of SSZ.20 in 1918.
Captain of SSZ.20 was Flt Sub Lt A.H.
Crump, shown in the bottom picture
looking back at the camera. The captain
of a 'Zero' flew his ship from the middle
cockpit, facing forward. In the front
cockpit was the W/T Operator whose
head can be seen to the left of the Lewis-
gun mounting.

Behind the pilot, directly in front of his
Rolls-Royce 75-hp 'Hawk' engine sat the
engineer, seen *in situ* in the top left-hand
photograph. Behind his head is the
radiator. In the top right photograph the
engineer is outside the car, standing on the
handling-rail. This was a common method
of communication between crew members.
Remember, they had no intercom as was
fitted to Second World War aircraft. They
had to pass written notes to each other or
else, if needing some exercise, get out onto
the handling-rail and edge along it until
level with the recipient – then lean
across and yell into his ear, while he
moved his helmet back to assist matters.
(*A.H. Crump via Ces Mowthorpe Collection*)

At least once in each 24 hrs, the top of a rigid airship had to be inspected by the Officer of the Watch or a Chief Coxswain to ensure that all valves and vents were clear and undamaged. This duty was carried out by walking along the walkway – a 2 ft wide strengthened gangway along the centre of the top of the ship. A 'walking-wire' was securely fastened for those of a nervous disposition! Most coxswains took great pride in walking upright without any support. Here we see Flt Sgt T. Parry returning from inspection of R.29 in 1919. Photographed by a fellow coxswain, he stands nonchalantly facing into the slipstream in front of the upper fin. He is wearing the 1919-type standard airship parachute harness – note the white strap around his legs. Parachutes were fitted to the keel of British airships in 1919 and, in the event of an emergency, the airshipman attached his harness to the parachute, then jumped out, dragging the parachute with him, thus opening it. (*Ces Mowthorpe Collection*)

A familiar situation for the early airships! Here, SS-39 is shown draped across houses at Thurlby, near Cranwell, in 1916. Engine failure caused the pilot to make a forced 'balloon landing'. Unfortunately, the wind blew his small airship over these houses and she snagged a chimney-pot. No one was injured, the houses were not damaged, and SS-39 was deflated, packed up and taken away by road transport. Re-inflated and re-rigged, she was flying again within a few days. (*By kind permission of Air Officer Commanding and Commandant of RAF Cranwell*)

CHAPTER ONE

The Pioneers

They flew. Did their duty. Then disappeared. The airshipmen. Today, millions of airline passengers travel eight or more hours in air-conditioned luxury. Thousands of airliners criss-cross the sky each day. Yet for fifty years prior to the Second World War, a special breed of flyers amassed considerable experience which can only be conjectured at today. There were fewer than five thousand, of which nearly half died sudden and dramatic deaths. These were the airshipmen.

Man's eagerness to fly like the birds was partially satisfied by the advent of the balloon. Unfortunately, balloons were not truly navigable. The invention of the lightweight petrol engine enabled a revised aerial machine to evolve. It took time and many experiments – some fatal. Finally a pattern emerged: elongated gas-filled envelopes, steerable rudders, elevators at the stern, and, suspended below, a car or gondola. Now it was possible to fly from one place to another with a reasonable chance of arriving safely. Because this contraption floated in the air – similar to a ship floating on the sea – it was given the name 'Airship'.

Eventually airships became huge monsters, big as ocean liners, crossing continents and oceans in their stride. These were the queens of the skies. Hundreds of smaller airships were built and flown, very successfully during the first forty years of the twentieth century. It is to the ingenuity, skill and bravery of their crews that this book is dedicated – the airshipmen. Try to imagine, sitting in an open fuselage, battered by a 40–50 mph wind in the icy blast of a propeller's slipstream (not for a short flight – eight hours was the norm during the First World War, often longer), unable to move and sitting a few feet below thousands of cubic feet of hydrogen. That was the position when everything was going smoothly – many times it did not! That was the working environment of an airshipman.

One of the best-known among the early pioneers was the Brazilian Santos-Dumont. Son of a wealthy father, he came to Paris in the 1891. After a balloon ascent in 1897, his fascination for aeronautics was fuelled, building his first airship, 82 ft long, shortly afterwards; then, opening a works and shed in 1901, at the Aero Club de France, Saint-Cloud, Paris. Here a further fourteen airships were built and flown with a modicum of success. His sixth, 103 ft long, with a 16-hp petrol engine and a capacity of 22,000 cu ft succeeded in flying from Saint-Cloud, around the Eiffel Tower and back again. The 9½-mile journey was completed in under half an hour thus winning Santos-Dumont a prize of 4,000 frs on 13 July 1901.

He built sixteen small airships in all. From his shed at the Aero Club de France at Saint-Cloud, Paris, he regularly rose and flew around the city, crashing on one occasion onto an apartment block. Unhurt, he climbed up the frame of the stricken machine, entered the apartment via a balcony window and calmly went down to the street and organised the salvage of his airship (No. 5) – to the cheers of an enthusiastic crowd. Perhaps his best remembered exploits was with his No. 9, a small single-seater airship of 1903. On a calm morning during that summer and late autumn, Santos-Dumont would often ascend from Saint-Cloud and fly across the Paris roof-tops, up the Champs-Elysées, or perhaps the Avenue de Bois-de-Boulogne, before alighting outside a pavement café where he had seen friends. Securing the airship to a convenient balcony he then

Santos Dumont sits on a ledge, surveying his collapsed airship. The framework is seen leaning up against the wall. Having already collapsed the envelope, he is endeavouring to salvage it with the aid of two curtain-rods, while onlookers peer down from the roof. (*Ces Mowthorpe Collection*)

Santos Dumont's No. 9. This small airship was very successful. He often flew it over and into the Paris streets, mooring it to a convenient balcony while he took coffee with his friends in a nearby café. Countess Aida d'Acosta persuaded Santos Dumont to teach her and allow her to fly this airship solo on one occasion. (*Ces Mowthorpe Collection*)

E.T. Willows pilots his
Willows 2 airship into
Cadogan Square, Birmingham,
in front of the city hall.
(*E.T. Willows*)

joined his friends for coffee before climbing back on board and taking off again. A lady-friend (Countess Aida d'Acosta), expressing great interest in how the controls worked, was instructed by Santos-Dumont. Then, one day, after further instruction, he allowed her to take the No. 9 for a short flight at Saint-Cloud. She was the first of the only two recorded women ever to have flown an airship solo, as pilot in charge.

As a point of interest, Santos-Dumont's No. 7, a small fast airship built to compete in the St Louis air race of 1904, was destroyed in its shed at Saint-Cloud – by vandals. That indicates that problems with law and order are not a recent phenomena.

Great Britain produced another pioneer, E.T. Willows, who performed similar feats at Cardiff, South Wales. Supporting the Cardiff Infirmary charity, he twice flew his small Willows 2 airship low over Cardiff and landed in Cadogan Square, near the City Hall, on 4 and 7 June 1910.

This same airshipman, accompanied by an engineer F.W. Goodden (who later achieved fame as an aeroplane test pilot) ascended from Wormwood Scrubs, London, on 4 November 1910, in his modified airship – now named *City of Cardiff*, en route for Paris. Crossing the

English Channel at night, the two intrepid aviators encountered fog, lost their maps overboard in the darkness and bedevilled by a number of mechanical faults, had to shut the motor off. Free-ballooning, the wind carried them into northern France, near Douai, where a forced landing was made. Repairs were carried out but before he could depart, a French Customs Official, together with gendarmes, requested £30 for 'the import of hydrogen gas'. Eventually, after a 24-hour delay, and agreement to depart French shores within a month, this duty was waived. Meantime, a storm had sprung up and the airship had to be deflated. Finally getting airborne on 15 November, the *City of Cardiff* suffered two more forced landings and a further deflation before finally arriving in Paris on 28 December 1910. Being the first airship to fly from England to France, cross the Channel in darkness and make the first direct London–Paris flight, the two flyers received a tumultuous reception. E.T. Willows remained in Paris giving flights around the Eiffel Tower for 200 frs but after applying to extend his visit, the French customs (who apparently had good memories) demanded he pay 743 frs per day or leave the country the next day! Deflating his airship, Willows, Goodden and airship, promptly returned to London – by rail.

Despite his many aerial accomplishments, the general public paid little attention to the name E.T. Willows, at least, in 1911. The then aeronautical world was more responsive. Having joined the Royal Aero Club as a founder member in 1906, he was selected to receive Airship Pilots' Certificate No. 4 when they were first issued on 14 February 1911. The other three selected were all leading military airship pilots: Col Capper, Capt Broke-Smith and Lt Waterlow. At the same time he was awarded Balloon Pilot's Certificate No. 19.

Time has forgotten Britain's earliest, and some would say greatest, airship pioneer, Ernest Thompson Willows. Apart from the above accounts which were arguably the high points in a sad life, E.T. Willows designed and flew six successful airships. Bear in mind the period, 1905–15. Flight of any kind was in its infancy, the only people in Britain designing and flying airships were the military at Farnborough. There, despite constant financial stricture, resources and equipment were available in abundance. On the other hand, E.T. Willows, the son of a comfortably-off Cardiff dentist, had no formal engineering training. Financially assisted by his father, he constructed sheds and built his airships – all leaders in their field. Shunned initially by the military aviators, he eventually sold them his No. 4 airship (which, when modified became His Majesty's

Airship No. 2). Although originally built with makeshift materials and under-powered, the 'experts' at Farnborough, over a period of time rebuilt the ship completely. Nevertheless when tested prior to purchase, Lt C.M. Waterlow (a noted military airship pilot) of the RFC – reported to his superiors: 'The features of the ship is its small size and general handiness; everything can be packed up and taken to pieces with the utmost care. For pleasure purposes this ship seems to be ideal. It would be very useful to train NCOs and men in handling on the ground and in the air.' As a result, the Admiralty bought the Willows No. 4 and while much modified, it rendered sterling service.

The key to Willows' successful airships was his control system. It was his own design, based upon the original idea of a Capt William Beadle, who had built an unsuccessful airship in 1903. Basically it enabled the propellers (one either side of the car) to be operated in any position from vertical to horizontal at the whim of the pilot, thus not only giving forward, but also vertical thrust. This principle of rotating propellers was later applied to many naval airships but eventually went out of favour. Following the Second World War, we have seen quite a revival of this useful feature.

The mechanical complication of rotating propellers was arguably the chief reason that Willows' sixth airship (a modification of his fifth) was not chosen for the SS-design for which it was submitted in 1915, alongside the successful Kingsnorth BE.2 fuselage/spare gasbag combination. The Navy wanted simple airships, easy to build and capable of being flown by quickly-trained young men. The SS-2 (Willows No. 6 airship) was very complicated. The rotating propeller system, although very efficient, proved too complex for mass production and was felt by the Navy to be an extra piece of equipment for inexperienced young pilots to handle.

The luckless E.T. Willows' life was full of thwarted ambition. Being an airships pioneer brought him two expensive court cases which he lost, bankruptcy, and disappointments at every turn. During the First World War he was associated with the Aircraft Manufacturing Co. Ltd, as Engineer and held a commission in the RFC. When hostilities ceased, he eaked out a living giving balloon passenger flights at various functions throughout the country. Sadly, on 3 August 1926, with four passengers in the craft, at the Kempston Flower Show, Bedford, the netting around his spherical balloon gave way and the five occupants plunged to their deaths: a tragic end to a plucky and clever pioneer airship-designer and pilot.

Throughout Europe, military authorities were experimenting with airships. In 1902, the enterprising airshipmen at the Royal Balloon Factory, Farnborough built Britain's first airship the *Nulli Secundus* which was moderately successful. Further experimental airships built at Farnborough were *Baby*, *Beta*, *Delta*, *Gamma* and *Eta*. None of these were really suitable for operational duties in wartime but did provide excellent experience for the airshipmen of what in 1911 became the Air Battalion of the Royal Engineers, with a military and naval wing. It was at Farnborough, during the building of the *Eta* in 1913 that perhaps the most important British contribution to non-rigid airships was made. Rigging an airship envelope to its cars (or gondolas) was a difficult task. If the envelope was too thin, it sagged in the middle. If too wide, it produced so much drag that control became difficult. Many different types of harnesses were developed but all had faults. Eventually at Farnborough, while building *Eta*, a system of multiple patches and bridles was evolved which so spread the weight of the car etc., that providing the centre of gravity was observed, anything could be attached to the envelope. Naturally this system became known as 'Eta Patches'. In similar form it was used world-wide for the attachment of anything, even fins and stabilisers to the airship's envelope.

Farnborough was twice the scene of almost a comic opera during 1910 and 1911, concerning the French 'Lebaudy' airship, bought by the British Government. The War Office had built a new airship shed at Farnborough to house the 'Lebaudy' (later known as the 'A-shed'), this was 10 ft higher than the dimension of the inflated airship. But, without notifying the War Office, the Lebaudy Brothers, builders of this vessel, increased the overall height by 9 ft 9 in! On 26 October 1910, following a successful non-stop flight from Paris with a crew of seven aboard, the 'Lebaudy' landed at Farnborough having been airborne for five and a half hours. Waiting to receive her was a ground crew of 160 guardsmen and sappers – plus a welcoming committee of 'top brass'. Manhandling the airship into its shed, the officer-in-charge realised that something was amiss and ordered a halt. Unfortunately, a brigadier present counter-manded the order! Under the impetus of 160 healthy young men the airship surged forward – promptly ripping the top of the envelope on the shed roof, and crashing, deflated, onto the ground.

This 'Lebaudy' was truly fated. It was rebuilt and taken out of its shed for a trial flight on 4 May 1911. Owing to modifications during rebuild, it soon became apparent that the airship was virtually

Two views of the fifth Zeppelin built at Friedrichshafen after a forced landing at Jebenhausen near Göppingen on 31 May 1909. Running out of fuel, the airship made a successful landing but due to the nose obscuring the only tree around from the helmsman, ran into said tree. Fortunately there was no wind so a hurried repair was made, the forward engine removed to save weight and the Zeppelin limped safely back to her shed at Friedrichshafen. (*Ces Mowthorpe Collection*)

uncontrollable! Rising to 600 ft, a number of erratic circuits were made. Coming in to land, too fast for the ground crew to hold her, the 'Lebaudy' careered across the airfield, crashing at high speed into a cottage on the boundary. Thankfully, there were no serious injuries, but the owner of the cottage claimed £4,000 damages which His Majesty's government refused to pay on the grounds that 'the airship was still owned by the manufacturers'. Payments to the airship builders or the cottage owner were never satisfactorily resolved as the outbreak of the First World War put a stop to all negotiations!

German airshipmen displayed considerable ingenuity on 31 May 1909. Count Zeppelin's fifth rigid airship had to make a forced landing at Jebenhausen, near Göppingen. The Zeppelin's nose impaled

One of the many home-built American airships which were flown between 1905 and 1912. This belonged to Charles Oliver Jones and was named *Boomerang. (Ces Mowthorpe Collection)*

itself onto a pear tree. Undeterred, the airshipmen carefully amputated the first three gas-cells – the Zeppelin had seventeen – drew the external covering over the open nose and 'tied it up'. Then the forward motor was removed to save weight. Thankfully the weather remained calm as they flew the 'foreshortened' and now single-engined Zeppelin safely back to Freidrichshafen.

Across the Atlantic, the exploits of Santos-Dumont, together with photographs, had been widely circulated by the Press. This led to a number of similar small petrol-engined airships being built by enthusiastic amateurs. Competitive trials between young aviators became an attraction at state fairs and similar, where 'Dirigible Races' became popular. St Louis, Missouri, held one in September 1907. Despite the lead that Europe possessed in lighter-than-air experience, similar events were not held on this side of the ocean.

These pre-1914 exploits, when airshipmen were few, are typical examples of the daring and initiative required by those who would fly the sky in large, fragile, hydrogen-filled gasbags. When war erupted, many more men would take to the skies – and more fascinating stories would emerge.

CHAPTER TWO

1914

The Royal Navy's involvement with airships goes back to the earliest days at Farnborough. Naval officers and other ranks had been on secondment, even though it was an Army base. As will be seen, these early airshipmen had no easy task.

In 1909 the Navy ordered a rigid airship from Vickers Ltd, formally named His Majesty's Airship (HMA) No. 1. Due to the successes of the early German rigid Zeppelins, it was felt that the Royal Navy should have a similar airship at its disposal. (Several attempts were made to buy a complete Zeppelin – not surprisingly, the German government refused to give the company permission to sell abroad.) During the fitting-out process the Admiralty specified quite unsuitable items for an airship: for example anchors, hawsers and even a capstan – all very heavy and completely useless in an airship! Typical naval slang gave HMA No. 1 a nickname, *Mayfly*, and this stuck. It was to be prophetic. The *Mayfly* was taken from her shed at the Cavendish Dock, Barrow-in-Furness and moored to a floating mast on 22 May 1911. Remaining at this mast for four days she survived gusts of 45 mph.

Her inflation with hydrogen had not gone without mishap. AB Palmer fell from the top of the airship, right through one of the gasbags, fortunately without serious injury. This falling from high up inside rigid airships was a hazard that befell a number of airshipmen, often causing serious injury. While aloft, where the lighter-than-air gas remained suspended, the poor riggers slowly suffered oxygen starvation due to a build-up of hydrogen from leaking valves and gasbags, thereby losing conciousness.

Returned to her shed, *Mayfly* was modified in an attempt to reduce her weight. The biggest change was to remove the keel which ran along the bottom, added to give strength. Rumours ran rife that thus weakened, she would break up in the air. Indeed a visible distortion of the hull was apparent.

His Majesty's Rigid Airship No. 1 – later designated HMA.1, but better known by her service nickname 'Mayfly'. After extensive modifications to lighten her, including taking away the keel, this picture shows the result of a gust of wind catching her while being drawn out of her shed at Cavendish Dock, Barrow-in-Furness. There also appears to have been mismanagement of the electric winches which pulled her outside. (*Ces Mowthorpe Collection*)

On 24 September 1911 she was eased from her shed for the second time, now using electric winches. Clearing the shed, she was struck by a gust of wind which laid her over almost on her beam-ends. As she righted herself, there was an ominous cracking and she broke in two – the crew leaping overboard.

Both halves were then gently eased back into the shed and broken up. Adm Sturdee (later to be victor of the Battle of the Falklands) was in charge of the Court of Inquiry. Viewing the remains he took one look, turned about and marched away, muttering – 'The work of an idiot!'

It is worthy of note that Cdr Maitland, one of Britain's leading airshipmen, was known to quote, in 1917, that 'Basically the *Mayfly* was a good design, ahead of its time. Had the Royal Navy persevered and built a small fleet of modified *Mayflys* in 1913, the Navy would have had a small rigid, with the capabilities of the much later North Sea class, at the outbreak of war.'

June 1914 saw the formation of the Royal Naval Air Service and the taking over of all Britain's airships and balloons. In typical naval fashion all the airships were correctly numbered, the ill-fated HMA No. 1 (*Mayfly*) starting the sequence. HMA No. 4 was the large non-rigid Parseval bought from Germany in 1912. By the outbreak of war, together with the similar Astra-Torres (bought from the French firm) HMA No. 3, these were the only two British airships suitable for war-service. Fortunately, there was now a core of experienced airshipmen operating within the Royal Naval Air Service.

Winston Churchill, First Lord of the Admiralty was very air-minded. Although favouring aeroplanes, he was enthusiastic about non-rigid airships because of their ability to patrol for long periods over the sea. On 23 October 1913, the Astra-Torres No. 3 was flown down to Sheerness under Captain Waterlow. Here, Winston Churchill came on board for a flight. His diaries state: 'I went in her for a beautiful cruise at about 1,000 ft around Chatham and the Medway. She is a very satisfactory vessel, and I was allowed to steer her for an hour. She was very easy to steer.' No doubt he recalled this flight when asked by his Admirals, in March 1915 for fifty Submarine-Searchers (plus 100 per cent spares), the RNASs first wartime airships.

The night before war was declared, the No. 3 and No. 4 were patrolling the Channel and its approaches. Returning to her war station at Kingsnorth, HMA No. 4 suffered the indignity of being mistaken for one of the much-vaunted German 'Zepps' and was fired at by a Territorial detachment stationed on the Kentish coast!

The German Parseval airships, of which HMA No. 4 was the eighteenth example, were powered by two 'Maybach' engines, each driving a four-bladed variable-pitch propeller. These propeller-blades bolted onto the propeller-hub and the Parseval company thoughtfully provided two spare blades, carried on board. On 15 August 1914, No. 4 was returning from an evening patrol, battling against an increasing headwind when one propeller-blade came off, fortunately without damaging the ship. Against the wind no headway could be made on one engine. Capt J.N. Fletcher was faced with having to drift backwards until over land, then carry out a forced landing at night. Coxswain Cook volunteered to unship the spare blades and, together with ERA (Engine Room Artificer) Shaw, proceeded to replace the broken blade. Completing the task ERA Shaw discovered that the new propeller-blade was lighter than the one opposite. Despite protests from Capt Fletcher, ERA Shaw insisted that to start the engine was unsafe unless he fitted the other spare blade opposite, to redress the balance. After a further 80 minutes they finally got under way. Darkness had fallen before these daunting tasks, carried out 1,500 ft above the sea, were completed. Meanwhile the airship, without power, had drifted well into Belgium. Coxswain Cook often told of how, as they eventually turned for home, the continuous flashes of gunfire, on what later became known as the Western Front, appeared almost below. Capt Fletcher confided in his crew after landing safely at Kingsnorth, that he had been prepared to destroy the

An illustration from *The Great War*, depicting Coxswain Cook and ERA Shaw changing the propeller of the P.4, 1500 ft above the Channel, while Capt Fletcher looks on. The date of this feat was 15 August 1914, and Coxswain Cook was awarded the DSM for his fine effort. (*from* The Great War *via* T. Jamison)

ship's papers and had soaked them in petrol – just in case! Coxswain Cook received the DSM for his meritorious conduct.

This adventure of HMA No. 4 is an excellent example of why, in 1914, airships were considered the best means of aerial navigation. When a crisis arose on an airship, it did not have to land immediately as would an aeroplane. Larger airships with two (or more) engines could still carry plenty of fuel, spare parts if required, and, by free-ballooning, these could often be fitted without landing – due to the efforts of the daring and ingenious airshipmen. Both No. 3 and No. 4 carried early radio transmitting and receiving sets as standard. Very few aeroplanes could even lift one of these early, relatively heavy pieces of equipment – and then only experimentally.

Nevertheless aeroplane performances were improving rapidly and while the advantages of airships were obvious, in wartime they suffered one serious disadvantage – they were large, slow-moving targets, especially over land! The Royal Navy however, viewed this 'disadvantage' rather differently. The relatively slow airship was two or three times faster than a surface vessel and if required it could slow down to a hover. Flying above the sea enabled them to spot any mines or U-boats in the path of shipping, long before surface lookouts.

All submarines or U-boats in use during the First and Second World Wars were in effect submersible boats. On the surface their speed was twice that of ordinary surface ships and this enabled them to move into an advantageous firing position ahead of their targets, their low profile in the water preventing them being spotted by ship's look-outs. Once ahead they submerged – where their speed was often less than that of their targets – but enough to manoeuvre into position for their torpedoes to strike home.

This fact on its own merited the use of airships. From their vantage point in the sky they could spot U-boats several miles away. With radio sets they could immediately call in surface forces to deal with the intruder. Trials carried out with British submarines before the war made the Navy aware that the simple presence of airships convinced a preying submarine's commander to submerge – rather than disclose its position. Due to the submarine's slow underwater speed it was then unable to get within range of its intended victims. These obvious facts were not, despite continual pressure from the RNAS lighter-than-air branch, fully understood by m'Lords at the Admiralty!

September 1914 saw the loss of three British light cruisers, HMS *Aboukir*, *Hogue* and *Cressey* in under two hours, sunk by the U-9 in the North Sea with a loss of 1,000 souls. Even this did not make m'Lords take the U-boat threat seriously. However, the loss of HMS *Formidable* to U-24 in the first few minutes of 1915 came as a nasty shock. Here, for the first time, a capital ship had succumbed to a submarine's torpedoes. Finally, steps to deal with this underwater menace were taken. One of these steps was to request the mass production of a fleet of small airships – each capable of 40–50 mph, with an endurance of eight hours, carrying a crew of two, 160 lb of bombs and a radio set, and capable of being flown by 'junior officers with small-boat experience'.

The Royal Navy issued specifications to two firms, Airships Ltd, where the designer was our old friend E.T. Willows, and Short Bros, aircraft and balloon manufacturers. The Navy's experimental base at Kingsnorth also submitted a design. Short Bros never did reply to the specification due to pressure of work, but later built many airships. Airships Ltd did build and fly an airship within six weeks – a modification of an existing model. However the design's complicated swivelling-propeller mechanism proved a stumbling-block to mass production as well as being a further burden upon the skills of the young inexperienced pilots.

At this period, early in 1915, the number of practical airshipmen in Great Britain was less than one hundred. Most had moved to RNAS Kingsnorth from Farnborough when the Navy took control of airships. Some were civilians, others ex-Army, but under the command of Cdr Masterman, RN, they became a team whose lighter-than-air experience and engineering capabilities were unsurpassed. Their ingenuity was boundless. The Navy needed a small airship quickly, so they took the fuselage of an aeroplane (a BE.2), dispensed with the wings and tail, attached it to an old 50,000 cu ft envelope of HMA No. 2 by means of their innovative '*Eta*-patches' (invented at Farnborough in 1913) – and there was a serviceable airship – flying on extended trials within a month of being specified! At the end of March 1915 the order was given for fifty similar ships to be built by the Navy, Short Bros and Airships Ltd, the latter two firms supplying different aeroplane fuselages but all with similar (originally) 60,000 cu ft envelopes.

These small airships were intended only for use in 'coastal waters' i.e. the Channel, Irish Sea and the Thames Estuary. Experience gained in these operations would form the foundation for larger, more efficient craft to follow. Of course the Navy had to find and train crews for these airships – and for the 200-plus which would be built during the remaining war years.

SS-4 free-ballooning after engine-failure near Warren, Folkestone. This is an excellent example of the pilot bringing-off a successful forced landing without damage to ship or crew. Note that the pilot and engineer are sitting on the outside of the 'car' in order to jump clear immediately the airship touches down. (*P. Liddle via JMB/GSL Collection*)

Initially the Navy asked for volunteers from the ranks of junior officers and selected seamen. Before acceptance they were induced by their COs to volunteer for 'Special Temporary Service of a Secret and Hazardous nature'. Volunteers were then posted to Wormwood Scrubs for training in ballooning, although the actual balloon flights took place from the Hurlingham Polo Ground. The reader must realise that if an airship had an engine failure – a not uncommon occurrence in 1915 – it, the airship, became in effect a balloon, and could safely be landed by a skilled balloonist.

In his book *Airship Pilot No. 23* (William Kimber), Capt Williams gives an excellent account of this early free balloon training. The RNAS had inherited a number of balloons when it was formed in 1914. Somewhere along the line they had all been given names. Probationary Flt Sub Lt Williams spent a month doing drill, knots and splices, rigging of non-rigid airships etc. Then, on 18 January 1916, from the nearby Hurlingham Polo Ground he made his first ascent in a coal-gas inflated balloon named *Swallow*, together with an instructor and three other budding airship pilots. They flew across London, passing St Paul's at 1,200 ft, and landing near Romford. Five days later in the balloon, *Shrimp*, they flew via Hyde Park to Mildenhall, in Suffolk. He notes that one of the pupils was reprimanded for trying to 'bomb' a double-decker bus near Marble

Arch with currant buns! Four days later a flight was made in *Seahorse*, which terminated in fog at Chingford.

On 1 February Sub Lt Williams passed out solo in the *Plover*, accidently rising in a thunderstorm to 13,000 ft, before landing safely near Aldershot. Due to bad weather his solo night flight in the *North Star* was delayed until 20 April when he succeeded in qualifying for his Aeronaut's Certificate No. 28 (dated 8 May 1916). Towards the end of February, SS-36 was attached to Wormwood Scrubs which gave pupils experience of powered flight while still carrying out balloon training. Finally, on 5 July 1916 Sub Lt Williams was passed out from RNAS Kingsnorth as a qualified airship pilot.

An interesting sidelight is told by Sub Lt Williams. A small, gold-beater's skin hydrogen balloon was kept at Wormwood Scrubs. Beneath it was suspended a simple plank, for a seat. Budding pilots were winched-up on this contraption to 'test their air sense'. Without any harness, it could be a frightening experience for a raw young aviator!

After qualifying, an airship pilot was moved to one of the newly commissioned 'war-stations' such as Polegate, Folkestone, Mullion or Anglesey, where he was converted into the mysteries of operational airship piloting by an experienced lighter-than-air pilot. During 1916, direct-entry pilots, from civilian volunteers was implemented and after qualifying at Wormwood Scrubs, they did two further courses, Navigation and Engineering, before being posted back to 'The Scrubs' where they carried out final training on balloons and airships. All First World War airship pilots were commissioned as Flight Sub-Lieutenants. Engineers and wireless operators were usually non-commissioned.

The late summer of 1915 saw a steady stream of new, virtually untried airships being flown by raw, eager, untried pilots. It could have been a recipe for disaster. Instead, the calibre, ingenuity and stubbornness of the rookie airshipmen – under the watchful eyes of disciplined, duty-conscious Royal Naval officers, brought about the birth of one of the Royal Navy's most successful anti-U-boat and mine-searching weapons.

CHAPTER THREE

The RNAS in the First World War

T he prototype of these small wartime airships — known as the SS-class, (SS standing for Submarine-Searcher or Submarine-Scout) — the SS-1, suffered destruction on its first flight to its war-station. Due to extended trials and modifications, prerequisites of all prototypes, it was not flown to the newly-commissioned RN Airship Station at Folkestone until 7 May 1915. The young pilot was Flt Sub Lt Booth (who went on to become one of Britains finest airship captains, eventually commanding the successful R.100). The inexperienced naval ground crew had laid out the 'Landing-Tee', a white T-shaped cloth indicating the wind direction to pilots, in the wrong direction. The long arm of the 'T' should point down-wind but, in their ignorance, they laid it pointing up-wind. Hence Flt Sub Lt Booth landed far to fast for the handling-party to grab his guy-ropes. Puzzled by his inability to slow down, Booth failed to notice some nearby overhead cables and on his third attempt flew into them. The resulting flash set fire to the escaping hydrogen and the SS-1 completely burned out. Fortunately, Booth and his wireless operator escaped with minor injuries.

Another problem which plagued these initial SS-ships was engines. The cars containing the engine and crews were modified aeroplane fuselages, complete with aeroplane engines. In 1915, an aeroplane had an engine running at high revolutions for relative short periods of under two hours. The speed of the aeroplane through the air at, say, 70 mph, ensured a cooling stream of air through the engine's radiator. An SS-ship flew at only half this speed and for well over four hours. Therefore the airship engines constantly over-heated and water-cooling pipes burst, causing loss of water or worse still, complete

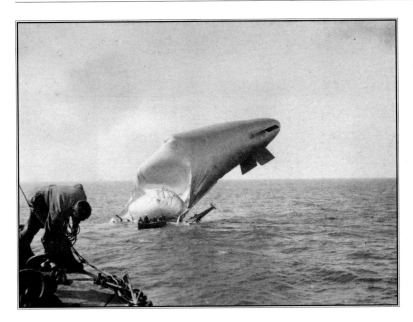

SS-10 after a forced landing in the English Channel during September 1915, due to engine failure. The crew were unharmed and the airship was successfully deflated and salvaged by the destroyer whose sea-boat had already taken off the two crew. SS-10 was rebuilt and re-numbered SS-10A, flying until late 1916 when she was again rebuilt and sold to the Italian Navy as the SS-10B, to spend many hours flying over the Mediterranean. (*Fleet Air Arm Museum*)

engines seizing-up. Gradually these mechanical shortcomings were overcome but in the meantime they gave our airshipmen many heart-stopping moments.

For example, SS-14, stationed at Mullion, Cornwall was re-engined with a special water-cooled American 'Curtiss', in an attempt to improve matters. This was to no avail. Poor Flt Lt C.E. Taylor and his wireless operator suffered a seized-up engine over the Channel on 7 September 1917. The wind was westerly as usual so for nearly six hours they drifted, or in RNAS parlance 'free-ballooned' up and across the Channel, finally crossing the coast of France where Flt Lt Taylor valved gas and made a safe landing.

Pilots and wireless operators became adept at re-starting engines in flight. Often when seen to be over-heating, the engine would be stopped and allowed to cool down. The intrepid wireless operator then climbed out of his cockpit and edged along the undercarriage skid while holding on to the car. Then, when within reach of the stationary propeller he would balance carefully, release one hand and swiftly flick the propeller-blade downwards. Usually the well-tuned engine burst into life and the W/T operator edged back into his cockpit. While all this was taking place the airship would be drifting with the wind, a thousand feet above the sea. Stopping and re-starting of the overheated engine could occur two or three times before reaching the safety of the land.

SS-17's maiden flight at Barrow, 3 July 1915, piloted by T.W. Elmhirst. Sent by rail to RNAS Luce Bay, together with SS-23, they pioneered operations from that station. Built by Vickers Ltd, SS-17 was the first successful airship to fly at Barrow. (*JMB/GSL Collection*)

Flt Lt Elmhirst had an alarming experience in SS-17 during the summer of 1915, while flying out of RNAS Anglesey. This time it was not engine failure but rudder cables which came adrift – leaving the pilot without directional control. Despite the crew's continual efforts to carry out repairs, the SS-17 free-ballooned right across the Irish Sea until a safe landing was made on the Emerald Isle. In order to reach the Irish shore they had to jettison all unnecessary equipment, even the wireless-set because they were slowly losing gas through a faulty valve.

SS-22 caused a minor sensation in Italy during September 1917. After service with the RNAS she was overhauled and sold to the Italian government. Re-assembled at Grottaglie, SS-22 suffered engine failure but was brought safely down by valving some of her gas. However, the Italian crew failed to secure her when they jumped out. Relieved of the crew's weight, SS-22 shot skywards, rising eventually to 10,000 ft where she was shot down by three Italian Nieuport fighter planes. The envelope, riddled with bullet-holes allowed the remaining gas to escape slowly, thus bringing the craft gently to earth. After repairing the envelope (and engine) this little airship flew many more voyages.

SS-40 was fitted with an enlarged (70,000 cu ft) black envelope and specially silenced engine. Under the command of Lt W.P.C. Chambers and Sub Lt Victor Goddard she operated out of a makeshift airfield at Boubers-sur-Canche close to the Western Front. Their story is worth telling.

Lt Chambers, captain of SS-13 at Capel was approached by Lord Trenchard, CO of the RFC in France during the spring of 1916 to volunteer for 'Secret Service in Enemy Territory'. Asked to recommend another airship pilot he chose his friend Sub Lt Victor Goddard, Captain of SS-12, also at Capel (later AM Sir Victor Goddard, KCB, CBE, RAF Retd).

They assembled SS-40 in a guarded hangar at Polegate and were soon ready for acceptance trials by the War Office. Apart from being the owners of the airship, m'Lords at the Admiralty washed their hands of the whole affair. One night towards the end of June 1916, in front of a general and his staff officers the all-black airship was hauled out for the first time. A successful but eventful maiden flight took place (the rudder cables jammed and the pilots had only limited control – fortunately the General and his officers were unaware of this!). One was heard to remark 'The ship became invisible as soon as she took off. Seemed to go round in a circle and fade away. Never saw her again until she landed. Very good show.'

By this time the pilots had been told the purpose of it all. SS-40 was to land and pick up Allied agents from enemy territory because their traditional route through neutral Holland had become unsafe. One modification was the fitting of a hand-operated pump to keep the envelope up to pressure (a tiring task when wearing full flying-gear), when the engine was cut, allowing the airship to drift back across the lines, aided by the prevailing wind.

Their base in France was at Boubers-sur-Canche, near Arras where a special airship hangar had been built by the RFC. Described by Victor Goddard as a 'cathedral of wood and wire covered by camouflaged canvas', it stood alone in a field close to a wood. SS-40 flew in on 2 July 1916 and two observer officers were allotted. Captains C.R. Robbins and A.N. Grieg, MC. Neither had any aerial experience whatsoever. Lt Chambers, the senior pilot was briefed personally by Maj Gen Trenchard at his HQ and upon his return a council of war took place between the four airshipmen. Loaded with all her equipment etc., SS-40 was unable to rise above 1,500 ft, normally an adequate height. Trenchard, however, had insisted that they were not to cross the lines at less than 10,000 ft – a sensible precaution. Signals were passed back to Polegate and it was decided that Sub Lt Goddard would fly the ship back for modifications. In the meantime, night-flying practice took place around the airfield.

Back at RNAS Kingsnorth, the envelope was enlarged to a capacity of 85,000 cu ft. The envelope was slit along its top surface and an extra gore (a wide piece of tapered fabric running from stem to stern) inserted. When re-inflated the airship had an expected ceiling of 13,000 ft. She was flown back to Boubers-sur-Canche on 10 August 1916 and upon arrival a further problem arose. She was too big to enter the shed! Frantically the base of the shed was excavated – all hands were pressed into service – half holding the airship secure on the field while the rest dug. At half-hour intervals they changed over. By dawn next day the airship had entered the shed.

It was now discovered that there was no requirement for dropping agents in enemy territory. Experiments dropping unmanned parachutes and releasing carrier pigeons were carried out on the night of 15 August 1916. During the later stages of the Battle of the Somme (August and September 1916), many aerial reconnaissances were carried out 'over the lines'. The envelope was punctured on many occasions by rifle bullets from our own troops when the airship was flying low on her return to base. This hazard was reduced by the crew singing bawdy songs at the top of their voices when flying below 1,000 ft. In his memoirs, the late AM Goddard records that the ship's return was heralded by a faint but increasingly loud rendering of *Three German Officers crossed the line, Skiboo, Skiboo etc., etc.*, (or similar) followed by the muffled sound of the throttled-back engine. Finally, out of the darkness crept the dark hulk of SS-40 into the hands of her handling party. Thankfully this hazardous venture was curtailed and SS-40 returned to normal duties in October. A postscript to this unusual task was that both pilots were mentioned in dispatches in General Haig's report on the Battle of the Somme.

Flt Sub Lt Cripps and his W/T operator tragically lost their lives in August 1917 while operating out of RNAS Pembroke. Arriving over base in the dark, having flown against an increasing head-wind, they made several attempts to land. Lack of airfield lighting disoriented the pilot, who was no doubt fatigued by nearly eight hours flying, and the little airship hit buildings on an adjacent farm. The propeller shattered and parts of the engine broke away. Relieved of this weight SS-42A lurched skywards and was carried out to sea, never to be seen again.

Not only were the flying-men in danger. Until either flying or safely in its shed an airship can behave most erratically. Those descriptive words 'lighter-than-air' mean just that. Hence, it is weightless – or almost so – immediately prior to, and immediately after, each flight, the slightest breeze causing potential danger to the ground-handling party when the huge monster writhes at the handling-guys. Many ground crews have been lifted high into the air, hanging onto the guy-ropes, and, if control was lost, carried away with the ships until they fell to their deaths, unable to hold on any longer. One of Britain's pioneer airship pilots and most experienced airshipmen Wg Cdr Waterlow always persistently drummed it into his men: 'Never hang onto the guy-ropes if lifted off your feet – let go immediately. Once airborne the airship is the responsibility of its pilot.' Ground-handling parties for the small SS ships numbered between fifty or sixty men, even in calm conditions. Sad to relate, Wg Cdr Waterlow disregarded his own maxim on 12 May 1917. SS-39 had suffered a defective valve and made an uncontrolled descent, landing in a tree at RNAS Cranwell, still containing a considerable amount of gas. While wreckage was being cut out of the branches, it suddenly broke free. All the rest of the party released except Wg Cdr Waterlow who was carried up until he fell to his death. By a sinister coincidence, his batman – assisting on this same airfield – died under almost identical circumstances a short time later.

Airshipmen were innovative to the extreme. One of the problems in shooting down a German Zeppelin was that by the time an aeroplane (in 1915) had climbed up to the same altitude as the Zeppelin, the Zeppelin had flown far away. Brainchild of Cdr N.F. Usborne and Lt Cdr de Courcy W.P. Ireland was the 'Airship-Plane'. A complete machine-gun equipped BE.2c aeroplane, slung beneath the envelope of an SS airship. As one unit, this 'Airship-Plane' would

AP-1, an 'airship-plane' designed by Cdr W.P. Ireland and Cdr Usborne to combat the Zeppelin threat. It was proposed to float an aeroplane to the attackers' height, then detach the aeroplane – leaving the envelope to descend by an auto-valve. Here, it is being test-flown by Lt Hicks at Kingsnorth, August 1915. The second flight of AP-1 by Cdrs Usborne and Ireland was fatal. (*Ces Mowthorpe Collection*)

Coastal C.6 at RNAS Pembroke. The twin-engined Coastals were the workhorses of the RNAS and the first truly 'operational' British airships. It was on these and the earlier SS-ships that the many problems which be-devilled the early airshipmen were solved, thus leading the way to superior classes of non-rigid airships. (*S.E. Taylor via Brian Turpin*)

rise and float at the height of the incoming Zeppelins. Once these were sighted, the BE.2c aeroplane would start its engine, operate a specially designed quick-release gear, then fly and attack the enemy: basically a sound idea. Known as the AP-1 this hybrid craft was prepared and successfully tested, without a live crew on board. Delighted, Usborne and de Courcy Ireland made a 'live' drop on 21 February 1916, flying the BE.2c themselves. Sadly, the release mechanism became entangled and the aircraft plunged to earth, its occupants being thrown out. This brought to a close what was both a clever and gallant lighter-than-air counter-weapon.

RNAS Kingsnorth's team of airship-engineers designed a larger, twin-engined airship to complement and build upon the experience gained with the small SS-ships. Three times the gas capacity, they were named 'Coastals' and carried a crew of four or five. Their endurance was originally eight hours but as they improved and experience was gained, up to twelve hours was possible. By late summer of 1915, the first Coastals began to arrive at their war-stations.

Pity the poor crews, imprisoned in their open cockpits in the slipstream – often icy – without any relief for up to eight hours at a time. Although wrapped in several layers of woollen underclothing and with sheepskin lined leathers outer garments, they often had to be bodily lifted out of the car during winter months and supported, until their frozen limbs regained control.

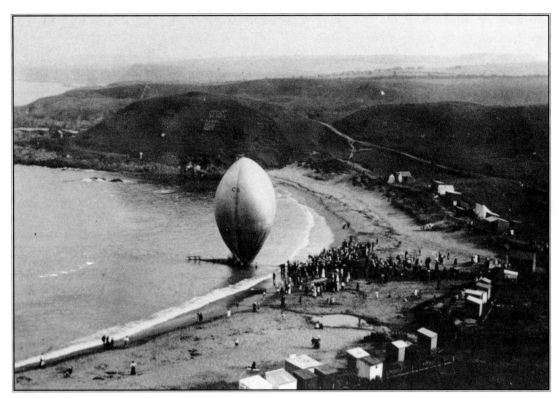

C.16 is here seen being salvaged in Coldingham Bay near Berwick, after both magnetos failed on both engines whilst on patrol. Fortunately the pilot was able to free-balloon towards land because he had a favourable wind. All crew were saved but the airship was a total wreck and struck off charge, later being replaced. (*Fleet Air Arm Museum*)

Although the engines of these Coastals were a great improvement on those of the earlier SSs, problems still arose. The worst was with magnetos. Prior to war breaking out in 1914, the German firm of Bosch supplied magnetos for internal combustion engines throughout Europe, including Britain. When hostilities broke out, each country naturally had to produce their own. This was not an insurmountable task, but the expertise which had grown up with the Bosch product was sadly lacking. It showed up in the unreliability of the early British magnetos. By 1918, the British product was as good as any in the world, but initially it was a different story.

Coastal C.16 was typical. After trials at RNAS Kingsnorth she flew to her war station at East Fortune, via Cranwell and Howden. Embarking on her first war patrol on the 28 August 1916 C.16 flew over the North Sea. After two hours she suffered magneto failure in one engine. Turning towards the coast her other engine stopped; again magneto trouble. Fortunately, the wind blew her shorewards and a successful forced landing was made in Coldingham Bay near Berwick. Because she was an airship and could still stay aloft while engineless, C.16 brought her crew safely home and they could explain the engine failures. How many aeroplane pilots were lost at that period through faulty magnetos? We shall never know.

It became the custom for airships to carry several spare magnetos during off-shore patrols. When one failed, the engineer had to wait for the engine to cool down, climb out of his cockpit and, sitting astride the engine, change magnetos, re-timing the engine afterwards, while the captain of the airship maintained station on the other engine. Up to three magneto changes during one single patrol has been recorded.

The crew of C.8 attempted an endurance record for RNAS non-rigid airships on 2 June 1916. The poor airshipmen got more than they bargained for! Due to engine failure in the vicinity of the Isle of White, they had drifted for four hours, until this was remedied. Limping back to the coast on one engine, an emergency landing was made at RNAS Polegate after 14 hrs 15 mins. This easily broke the (then) record – but because of the enforced 'free-ballooning' – did not count!

Sister-ship C.9 claimed this record in the following month with a trouble-free flight of 19 hours, covering 320 miles. It was rather spoilt when C.9 ran out of petrol and force-landed in the sea, two

C.9 secured at Mullion Cove after her record flight in July 1916. Out of fuel, within sight of her base RNAS Mullion, C.9 was taken in tow by a destroyer and left as shown. Fuel was brought from base, engines re-started, envelope blown up to pressure and her pilot, Flt Lt Struthers, flew her back to base. (*Peter London*)

miles from shore. Fortunately a passing destroyer took her in tow, disembarking her with only slight damage. Most of C.9's life was under the command of Flt Lt Struthers, who, through sheer dedication and skill, took a major part in the destruction of three U-boats.

C.9's most significant achievement occurred on 3 October 1917, after escorting a convoy. Returning to RNAS Mullion from a long, tiring patrol and fighting a rising wind, her W/T operator heard a distress call. Looking astern they saw one of the ships had been torpedoed near Start Point. Flt Lt Struthers wheeled round smartly and, aided by a now following wind, sped towards the scene. A diligent search spotted the U-boat's periscope, slightly ahead. When directly overhead, the airship dropped her four 110-lb 'depth-bombs'. Bubbles of air came to the surface indicating that the enemy was at least badly damaged, and C.9's wireless operator signalled a nearby armed trawler for assistance. The armed trawler attacked with depth-charges, the U-boat being presumed sunk. Meanwhile, Flt Lt Struthers was forced to leave the scene due to shortage of fuel, and resume his flight back to Mullion against deteriorating weather.

Flt Lt Hogg-Turner was unlucky on 23 April 1917. Returning to RNAS Howden from an early patrol in C.11, he crossed the coast near Scarborough. It was one of those mornings when the air was still and a coastal mist – known locally as a 'sea fret' – was slowly rising over the town, still shrouding the top of a well-known hill called Oliver's Mount. Conscious of this hill, concentrating upon avoiding it in the swirling clouds, Hogg-Turner edged over to the west. Unfortunately the mist concealed more high ground – Racecourse Hill. Suddenly C.11's car struck this obstruction at 50 mph! The airship-car broke in two, depositing a somewhat surprised engineer and his rear engine on the ground! Meanwhile the airship, relieved of this weight, shot skywards into the cloud. Hogg-Turner's controls were virtually useless so in desperation he pulled the emergency rip-cord. This brought about rapid deflation of the envelope and now, instead of rising, the remains of C.11 began to descend – rather smartly. Emerging from the 'sea fret', airship and its remaining occupants fell violently into the grounds of Scarborough College, seriously injuring Flt Lt Hogg-Turner, his Coxswain and W/T Operator. Fortunately these gallant men all recovered. What of our Engineer? Deposited with one of his engines upon Racecourse Hill he staggered to his feet and made his way to an adjacent road. Taking directions from a farm labourer, he commenced to jog-trot into

Scarborough's suburb of Falsgrave. Here he located the post-office and after much difficulty, because he had no money, persuaded the post-mistress to send a telegram to RNAS Howden explaining matters. He was not the only airshipman to find that post-mistresses were not sympathetic to penniless, fallen aviators!

The remains of Coastal C.11 were dispatched by rail back to RNAS Howden. Here it was rebuilt as the C.11A and took to the air for trials on 21 July 1917. Sadly, this fated airship burst into flames over the river Humber and was destroyed, with fatal consequences.

As defence against attack by enemy aeroplanes, these Coastal's had a machine-gun platform on the top of the envelope. One of the crew, usually the engineer, was trained to use this weapon. Getting to this gun-position meant climbing-up a rope ladder enclosed in a canvas tube, passing completely through the airship's envelope, emerging on the top where a small wooden platform carried a Lewis-gun on a simple mounting. Theoretically a sound idea, but in practice there was the ever-present possibility that sparks from the firing gun could ignite hydrogen-gas leaking from a faulty valve – thus blowing the airship apart! Hence, most airship captains left this platform unmanned, saving weight by leaving the weapon and its appendages behind. Interestingly, many German Zeppelin captains had arrived at the same decision for the same reason!

Thus on 21 April 1917, Flt Sub Lt Jackson and his crew in C.17, patrolling near the North Hinder Lightship – the extreme eastern edge of their sector, and midway between East Anglia and Zeebrugge – were defenceless when attacked by German seaplanes, led by Cdr Christianson. The speed of the attack prevented any signals being sent, and RNAS Pulham was unaware of C.17's fate until the German radio announced their victory, several days later. Sadly, the Station-Paymaster, Comm. W/O Walters, had gone along on this patrol, 'just for the ride' and was lost with the crew. After this the Admiralty insisted upon the upper machine-gun being manned at all times while flying over the sea, even when it meant carrying an extra crew member. Tragically C.27, (Flt Lt Kilburn) fell to the same German seaplanes on 11 December 1917, despite her operational gun position.

The Rigid Trials Flights Parsevals P.5 and P.6, operating out of RNAS Howden took this instruction to the extreme. These Parsevals had no upper gun position. One was immediately installed, together with a machine-gun position on the nose – irreverently called 'the Howden pulpit'. Gunners crawled along a canvas tube beneath the envelope and after emerging at 'the pulpit', the upper gunner attained his position by climbing the rope ladder affixed to the nose of the airship. Both guns were continuously manned whenever the airship was flying over the North Sea.

Indirectly the fate of C.27 led to the loss of another Coastal, C.26. Her captain was Flt Lt Dixon. His closest friend was Flt Lt Kilburn, captain of C.27. So upset was Flt Lt Dixon at his best friend going 'missing' that he persuaded his CO to allow C.26 to search the area next day – despite marginal weather conditions. Searching desperately for some sign of C.27 and her crew, their comrades in C.26 stretched the flight to its maximum limit. Finally turning for base, Flt Lt Dixon ran out of fuel before reaching the English coast. At the mercy of a rising storm the airship was blown across to Holland where it landed safely near Dordrecht. As the crew leapt to the ground, the airship, thus lightened, broke away, finally coming down at Eemses, near the Zuider Zee. As Holland was a neutral country, the crew were interned until the end of the war.

Another Coastal and crew were lost in rather mysterious circumstances. C.25, commanded by Flt Lt Hopperton was on patrol from East Fortune on 29 July 1918. With two other airships she was directed to search for a damaged U-boat in the area. She reported her position at 1840 hrs by wireless, but a further attempted transmission broke up abruptly. Nothing further was

Parseval P.6 at RNAS Howden, May 1917, after being fitted with an upper gun position plus one situated right on the nose – known as the 'Howden Pulpit'. Unlike the Coastal-class, whose gunner climbed an internal tube inside the envelope, the Parsevals had no such tube. Hence the gunners climbed into the external tube below the envelope from the car, emerging in the nose 'pulpit'. The upper gunner then climbed up over the nose on the external rope ladder, to his position. Fortunately, these weapons were never fired in anger. (*Ces Mowthorpe Collection*)

C.27 falling in flames after being attacked by German seaplanes on 11 December 1917. Although her upper gun was manned, it was to no avail. German seaplanes operated out of Borkum and at extreme range they overlapped the furthest edge of the RNAS airships' patrol area near the Kentish Knock light. Had C.27 turned for base a few moments earlier, this encounter would have been averted. There were no survivors. (*JMB/GSL Collection*)

These two pictures show the extensive modifications carried out by the crew of C.25 to their airship in an attempt to improve efficiency. This was a station modification done with the CO's full approval. No other Coastal airship was similarly modified. (*Royal Aeronautical Society*)

heard of C.25 until one of her propellers was found floating in the area some days later. After the war it emerged that the U-boat, limping home on the surface and unable to dive had engaged 'an airship' with its deck gun, scoring a direct hit. Shortly after its distorted wireless signal reported this engagement – the U-boat sank without trace. C.25's crew were so enthusiastic about their flying that they had carried out extensive modifications to C.25's car in order to improve efficiency.

U-boat crews were brave men and like their comrades in the Second World War were prepared to 'fight it out' on the surface – if need be. They soon discovered that an airship was a large slow-moving target – under certain conditions. The explosive shells of their deck gun must have been a terrifying experience for airshipmen, suspended beneath thousands of cubic feet of hydrogen. In the Mediterranean, several of the SS-class airships operated against German U-boats but had only a limited use. Their engines never developed maximum power, due to the climatic difference. One ex-U-boat commander wrote in the 1920s that 'on his several encounters with British airships, he had steamed at full speed *into wind* – easily out-pacing his enemy – while engaging them with his deck gun.'

The Airship Expeditionary Force in the Eastern Mediterranean came about through the Gallipoli landings. This was followed by the Allied expedition to Salonika and the evacuation of the Gallipoli Peninsula. U-boat activity was always present but initially, experiments were carried out with spotting for land and sea-based naval guns. These Mediterranean operations were never completely successful, although, in the clear Aegean waters, mines could effectively be located. Airships were based at Mudros on the island of Lemnos and a forward out-station at Imbros. Later a new station was laid out at Kassándra on the Khalkidhiki peninsula.

Conditions in the warm moist air taxed the efforts of both airships and airshipmen. Despite superhuman efforts, it was almost impossible to keep more than two of the five SS-airships serviceable at any one time.

Constantly harassed by Turkish aircraft these airshipmen generally had an uncomfortable life. 24 October 1916 found SS-8 and her crew being attacked by a Turkish seaplane. Incendiary ammunition was still unknown and the method used was for the seaplane to climb over SS-8 and drop bombs onto her envelope. Fortunately, neither of the two attacks were successful, the bombs falling clear astern. By mid-1917, Turkish reversals on the Eastern Front brought out an Admiralty scheme for one of the Mudros airships to be fitted with bomb racks and an attempt to bomb Constantinople. It was a non-starter. The airships were so depleted of power by climatic conditions that they could scarcely lift themselves, let alone bombs. This scheme had an interesting sequel. One of the early Handley-Page O/100 twin-engined bombers was brought out and assembled. It

This Coastal Star 6 shows well the new Coastal Star-class streamlined envelope in contrast to the blunt hump-backed envelopes of the original Coastal-ships. Many other modifications were incorporated and the result was a fine airship. Built as a stop-gap until the snags with the larger North Sea class had been corrected, the Coastal Stars rendered excellent service with no losses. Here, Coastal Star 6 is on patrol 400 ft off the Cornish Coast. (*Fleet Air Arm Museum*)

carried out the proposed bombing missions until lost in an accident on 30 September 1917. These Handley-Page missions were the first transcontinental bombing raids ever undertaken.

Throughout the eastern Mediterranean, anti-U-boat and mine patrols were undertaken, and much experience was eventually gained. Had the Armistice not intervened, reinforcements of the latest SS-Zero airships would have given much improved service.

Coastal airships and their crews were the workhorses of the airship service and an improved version was built – the Coastal Stars. During 1918 two little-known schemes were hatched to extend the Coastal Star's activities. A small circling-torpedo, for use against U-boats was being developed and it was planned to drop these from airships. Also, plans were afoot to use them as aerial-ambulances to transport seriously injured soldiers from the Western Front while heavily escorted by fighter aircraft. The Armistice came before either were operational.

By now (1917) the experienced Royal Naval airshipmen were constantly seeking to improve their ships. The SSZ (Zero) was in truth, a private venture started at RNAS Capel. Cdr A.D. Cunningham, Lt E.M. Rope and WO Righton designed and built this brilliant little airship without any official backing – a lapse which brought them much embarrassment – they were severely reprimanded for the 'improper use of Admiralty time and materials'! While the twin-engined Coastals and North Sea class were excellent ships in themselves, it was felt by airshipmen that a 'twin-engined

Here, the prototype of the Mullion Twin (later designated SSE-2, and still later SST-1 – all the same airship) is seen in the River Pym after an emergency landing during a rising gale. (*Fleet Air Arm Museum*)

Zero' would be much more efficient. This time, the Admiralty was brought in early and the venture became official. The airship depot at Wormwood Scrubs developed one design, RNAS Mullion developed another. Mullion won. Their 'Mullion Twin' became officially SS.Twin-1 and thirteen became operational before hostilities ceased. Another example of the airshipmen's ingenuity but, as the photograph shows, it was not without difficulties.

Airshipmen, like their sailor comrades-in-arms were a superstitious lot. On at least two occasions RNAS Pulham redesignated airships numbered 13 to 14A! This also occurred at RNAS Kingsnorth.

CHAPTER FOUR

The Final War Years

Late 1916 saw the airship firmly established as a major weapon in the war at sea. Two years' experience found airshipmen rapidly becoming masters of their craft. The early pioneers were now in charge of RNAS airship stations or similar positions. Their knowledge had been passed on to the RN officers and seamen who had originally volunteered to fly the SS-ships and Coastals, while a direct-entry scheme for civilian volunteers was well under way.

May 1916 saw the only major sea battle between two modern, big-gun battle fleets, at Jutland. Due to extremely skilful manoeuvres, the German Adm von Scheer evaded a crushing defeat, returning his battered ships safely into port. Erroneously, much credit for this was attributed to scouting German Zeppelins. In fact, no aircraft of either side was present (with the exception, for a brief

NS-12 is a good example of what many airshipmen believe to be the finest non-rigid airship of its time. The early North Seas developed serious trouble with their propeller drive-shafts. Production was stopped and the Coastal Star substituted. However, after six months of trials, this problem was overcome and during 1918 they performed sterling work. All accommodation was enclosed and they carried a crew of ten (two watches of five each) and could fly without landing for up to two days. (*Royal Aeronautical Society*)

spell, of a Royal Naval Short Seaplane) but the following morning crews saw Zeppelins lurking at extreme range and these were believed, quite wrongly, to have used radio signals to guide the German High Seas Fleet through the Royal Navy's ships during the night, after the battle. The outcome was that, suddenly, after years of indecision, the Royal Navy wanted rigid airships, just like the Zeppelins. Naturally this would take some years to achieve. In the meantime, more modern types of non-rigids would not only search the seas for U-boats and mines, but actually work as scouts, with the surface fleets.

The Royal Navy, capable as ever, took this rapid expansion in its stride. The large rigid airships, were built by private firms such as Vickers, Armstrong-Whitworth and Beardmore. The naval design team at Kingsnorth had already built a large non-rigid design, which was the North Sea Class, capable of staying aloft for two days. Each North Sea class airship carried a crew of ten – two complete crews – with basic accommodation. Initially, fifty of this class was ordered but owing to a serious design fault holding up development, only twenty were built.

As already quoted, at RNAS Capel, near Folkestone, the CO, Cdr A.D. Cunningham, one of the truly enterprising pioneers, was working with his engineering officer Lt F.M. Rope (later to lose his life in the R.101 disaster) and WO Righton on the design of a small, but efficient airship to replace the primitive SS-ships. This design work did not disrupt RNAS Capel's wartime duties, but fitted in around them. The result was the SSZ (Zero) class, a three-seater, powered by a purpose-built Rolls-Royce 'Hawk' 75-hp engine. It was a superb little airship: eighty-odd were built before hostilities ceased in November 1918. Besides these two major classes, several other designs were under way.

The crews for this influx of airships came almost entirely from civilian volunteers, brought into the RNVR as probationary pilots, attaining the rank of flight sub-lieutenant upon completion of training. Training schools were expanded and RNAS Cranwell, in Lincolnshire (later to become the RAF college), was built as the world's first purpose-built flying training school. Not only airship pilots were trained – directly opposite, on the other side of the huge grass airfield was a contemporary training facility for RNAS aeroplane pilots. This vast naval investment in pilot training was the true birth of the huge Empire Training Schemes, twenty-five years later, during the Second World War and indeed, together with the

Here SSZ-42 (a Zero-class airship) is seen landing at Laira, a mooring-out site belonging to RNAS Mullion, in Cornwall. These 'Zeros', as they were popularly known, were extremely efficient little airships. Easily handled by an inexperienced pilot, they instilled confidence which, together with their beautiful Rolls-Royce 'Hawk' engines, meant they were much-loved. Their boat-shaped cars were waterproof and could be put down on water. A crew of three – pilot, W/T operator and engineer – regularly performed flights of up to 10 hours. (*Fleet Air Arm Museum*)

RFC Gosport School of Flying, forms the true background of every professional aircraft pilot flying today.

Some idea of the advance that had taken place can be appreciated when it is known that the first of the North Seas, NS-1, under the command of Lt Cdr Robinson, made a flight of 49 hrs 22 mins (1,536 miles) in June 1917: a world record for non-rigid airships. NS-2 was not so fortunate. On her second flight (27 June 1917) she had to force-land at Stowmarket and was completely wrecked – luckily without serious injury to her crew. Production was stopped until 1918 when the faults were corrected and this excellent airship-class came into its own.

The first of the Zeros, SSZ-1 was a lucky ship. On 16 September 1918, under the command of an American, Ensign N.J. Learned (who had been seconded to the Royal Navy for airship pilot-training) she sighted an oil-slick from UB-103, and after calling up on W/T a patrol vessel, succeeded in destroying the enemy. Her sister-ship SSZ.2 was not so lucky. On 14 February 1917 while escorting transports to Boulogne, her engine failed and a destroyer manoeuvred beneath her to pick up her trail rope and tow her to safety. Unfortunately, SSZ.2 drifted over the funnels and the heat and sparks ignited the gasbag. Her crew of three leapt smartly overboard into the sea and were saved by the destroyer's seaboat.

Wreck of NS-2 at Stowmarket on 27 June 1917. This was the first sign of the serious fault in the propeller-drives of the original North Sea design. NS-2 carried out successful trials after assembly at RNAS Kingsnorth on 16 July 1917, but on her delivery flight a few days later, both propeller-drives broke. The resulting crash wrote off the airship but fortunately there were no casualties. As a result, production of North Seas was halted until a solution was found. (*Fleet Air Arm Museum*)

A tragic accident brought about the destruction of the SSZ.7 and SSZ.10, both belonging to RNAS Polegate. On the morning of 22 December 1917 five Zeros took off on anti-submarine patrols: SSZs 6, 7, 9, 10 and 19. A strong breeze from the north-east brought a dark, heavy fog along the coast and over the Downs. Radio signals recalled the five airships immediately. By the time they reached base, RNAS Polegate was completely covered with fog, so emergency landings were made in the countryside where better visibility still remained. SSZ.6 landed north of Hailsham, SSZs 7 and 19 found a clear spot on the cliffs by Beachy Head. However, Zeros 9 and

10 flew inland, landing near a farm at Jevington. So far all the craft were secure. Later that evening a rising wind started to clear the fog and the threat of a gale brought imminent danger to the temporarily moored ships.

Despite approaching darkness, drizzle and wind, each airship captain decided independently to make a dash for base at Polegate, where, forewarned by wireless, landing-lights had been laid out on the airfield. Flying low through the night, SSZ.6 was soon in the capable hands of a mooring party. SSZ.19 then appeared over the airfield and she too landed safely. However, it soon became apparent that things were not all right with the remaining Zeros. Wireless transmissions had been received; now there was an ominous silence.

SSZ.7 had lost touch with her sister-ship after leaving Beachy Head and unfortunately drifted towards Jevington. Her captain, Lt Swallow, peering over the side saw an Aldis light shining towards him. Thinking he was over Polegate and the Aldis a marker-beacon, he proceeded to descend. Tragically the Aldis was being wielded by the captain of SSZ.10, who had heard the low-flying airship – as a warning signal. This error was fatal. Descending near the shining light, the car of SSZ.7 smashed into the envelope of SSZ.10 releasing thousands of cubic feet of hydrogen and as Lt Swallow desperately opened his throttle to climb away, his hot exhaust caused a huge explosion which engulfed both airships. Two crew members dashed into the blazing wreckage and extricated the dead captain and his seriously-injured crewmen, then bravely returned and detached the two bombs before they exploded in the inferno. For this action, Air Mechanic Robinson and Boy Mechanic Steers both received the Albert Medal in gold.

Meanwhile SSZ.10's captain, Lt V. Watson, mistakenly thinking one of his crew was still inside, returned to his blazing ship to attempt a rescue – despite the imminent danger of exploding bombs. Seeing his ship had no crew, Lt Watson turned about and ran back. Just then the two 65-lb bombs exploded, seriously wounding him and blowing off his right arm. For this gallant action he received the Albert Medal in bronze. Thanks to the prompt action of her crew, the remaining Zero, SSZ.9, was safely moved away from the scene and subsequently made her way to base.

The Court of Inquiry into what became known as the 'Jevington Incident', involving the death of Lt Swallow, serious injury to Lt Watson and two crewmen, and the loss of two 'Zero-class' airships attributed the whole incident to 'sheer bad luck combined with appallingly difficult weather conditions'. Tight wartime security and censorship surrounded all things military at this period, so no public account was ever given. As a result, many myths and rumours have abounded about 'airships crashing and large numbers of casualties near Jevington' over the years. The foregoing is an accurate account based upon official sources.

SSZ.9, still at Polegate, had another adventure on 24 August 1918. Returning from patrol she flew into a strong north-westerly gale, running out of fuel just short of the English coastline. Her captain, Lt Morlebury, free-ballooned across the Channel and calmly pulled off a forced landing near Berthouville, south of Rouen, without injuring his crew or damaging the airship. Packing up the deflated craft, a return to RNAS Polegate was made via rail and boat. A week later SSZ.9 was again on patrol.

A light-hearted incident, which could have been serious occurred to SSZ.12, based at RNAS Luce Bay. The nearby seaside town of Stranraer was full of visitors on 18 July 1918 when the airship and crew were returning to base. A beautiful summer evening and a pier full of young ladies in short dresses tempted the pilot to do a 'chuck-up' – the airship equivalent of a 'beat-up'. At 50 mph, he flew across the end of Stranraer Pier – there was a flag-pole at its extremity! The SSZ.12 flew straight into this obstruction, piercing her envelope. Fortunately she was able to limp across to the beach before losing all her lift. An ignominious return to Luce Bay was made by rail!

Her sister-ship, SSZ.16, based at Pembroke, more than met her match over the Irish Sea on 7 December 1917. The crew, unlike many crews, actually saw a U-boat. It surfaced directly ahead of the airship. Steering straight for the enemy, the w/op – gunner in the front cockpit fired all his machine-gun ammunition at the enemy craft as they flew over. Not to be outdone, the U-boat commander manned his 3-inch deck gun and fired a dozen rounds at SSZ.16 before submerging again, as the airship circled around, her startled crew wirelessing for surface craft. The U-boat got away!

The reader will recall that when the C.11 crashed at Scarborough, the engineer had great difficulty in persuading the post-mistress to telephone his base of his dilemma. Something about airshipmen must annoy these guardians of our Royal Mail! In July 1918, SSZ.45 force-landed at Toller Down, near Bridport. The observer J. Owner was thrown out and sustained some injuries. The pilot H. Savage and engineer H. Jobson were quite seriously injured. Gallantly, J. Owner staggered over a mile to the nearest post office, where the post-

SSZ-45 at Toller Down, Dorset, after its forced landing – the envelope has been deflated. The Observer/WT operator, J. Owner, who was thrown out on impact, is standing, bare-headed, on the left. Pilot H. Savage and Engineer H. Jobson had been taken away by ambulance. (*JMB/GSL Collection*)

mistress was again most reluctant to make a free emergency call to the RNAS Mullion.

During the summer of 1918 experiments were carried out with the Royal Navy's new aircraft-carrier HMS *Furious*. Two Zeros, SSZ.59 and SSZ.60 operating out of RNAS East Fortune rendezvoused with HMS *Furious* off the Scottish coast and both airships made several landings on her flight-deck. Although successful, they were never repeated.

SSZ.65 celebrated the Armistice by making a record flight of 535 miles in 17 hrs 44 mins under the command of Lt Anderson. This illustrates the huge advances made with these small airships in a period of three years. Not only in the airships themselves but also in the crews, both air and ground, which made such a flight possible. The reader must appreciate that in the summer of 1918, few, if any, aeroplanes, could have achieved this endurance record, which the SSZ.65 carried out in the normal course of her duties.

Another unusual post-Armistice flight was that made by Lt Elmhirst in November 1918. During Armistice celebrations at the Anglesey airship station, Capt Gordon Campbell VC, RN, challenged Lt Elmhirst to fly them both beneath the Menai Bridge, which connected the island to the mainland. Accepting the challenge, Lt Elmhirst, the CO of RAF Anglesey, sent a car for the captain, on a calm morning some days later. Together, in SSZ.73, they achieved this remarkable feat. Remember, the pilot of an airship cannot see directly above because of the airship's envelope. What

Summer of 1918 saw the RNAS airships experimenting with working alongside the battle fleet. SSZ.59 and SSZ.60 landed on the flight deck of HMS *Furious*. Here we see SSZ.59 actually on the flight deck while SSZ.60 circles, awaiting her turn – meanwhile one of her crew recorded the event on camera. (*Ces Mowthorpe Collection*)

would be only a daring feat in an aeroplane becomes extremely hazardous in an airship. A Naval photographer recorded the flight.

The wartime airshipman, unlike his regular naval officer counterpart, had little experience of navigation, either aerial or oceanic. Airships usually operated close to shorelines, therefore true 'dead reckoning' was unnecessary. However, bad visibility meant that the airship pilot could be out of sight of land for several hours. Therefore, if he did not know his position, he would be unable to call up surface vessels should he sight the enemy. It was essential to find the speed and direction of the prevailing wind at the airship's operating height, their sheer size and relatively slow speeds making them very susceptible to 'drift'.

Airship pilots found an easy way to assess these two factors. Approaching a fixed point such as a buoy, lightship or pier, the airship was brought to the hover. Gradually ruddering until it was facing directly into wind, throttle was reduced and the craft brought to a standstill above the fixed point. Then his 'indicated airspeed' showed the wind velocity and the reciprocal of his compass heading, its direction. 'Taking the wind' at each end of his patrol line up the coast enabled the airshipman to accurately allow for drift and thus quickly estimate his time and distance from a pinpoint, should he need to radio for assistance. Rigid airships flying across oceans would drop a 'smoke float' into the sea and use this as a fixed point. Aeroplanes were unable to estimate the wind by this method.

Flt Lt Elmhirst flew his superior officer, Captain Gordon Campbell VC, underneath the bridge over the Menai Straits to celebrate the Armistice in November 1918. Flt Lt Elmhirst was CO at RNAS Anglesey, and his photographic section recorded the feat. (*AVM T.W. Elmhirst via Ces Mowthorpe Collection*)

Airships, compared to aeroplanes were in 1918 considered quite safe – there was no sudden plunge to earth if anything went wrong, they simply valved gas and landed like a balloon. But not always. On 29 August 1918 the brand-new SST.6 took off on her trial flight. At 400 ft it was noticed that smoke was coming from an engine. The conflagration grew and the flaming mass fell to the ground, killing Capts Rigton, Barlett and King, as well as Sgt Cameron and Air Mechanic Cowen. It all happened so quickly that at the Court of Inquiry no one watching could give a coherent explanation, and the resulting verdict: Accident caused by fire.

When the first North Sea class of airship flew in February 1917, high hopes of 'better times' in the airship service appeared possible. These fine ships had enclosed accommodation for two crews and were capable of staying aloft for up to 48 hours. Unfortunately, a design fault caused the loss of NS-2 and NS-5. Production was halted while modifications were made. By 1918, the North Seas were fully operational and much fine work was accomplished before the Armistice. Nevertheless, serious incidents could still occur.

The night of 21 June 1918 found NS-3 in serious difficulties. A rising wind left her captain, Flt Cdr J.C. Wheelwright, DSC, with no choice but to turn back to base. Battling against increasingly turbulent gusts of up to 40 knots her crew breathed a sigh of relief when the Isle of May was sighted at the entrance to the Firth of Forth. But all was in vain. Three miles off shore the NS-3 suddenly began to descend rapidly. With full power and the nose up she struck the sea, ripping off the two engine cars behind the control car. The loss of weight caused the remains to rise 500 ft until loss of hydrogen caused them to crash back into the sea. Second pilot P.E. Maitland (later Air Vice-Marshal, RAF) relates how Capt Wheelwright turned to his coxswain, PO Hodgson, shook his hand and said 'Goodbye' just before they struck. Scrambling out of the wreckage and swimming to the deflated, but floating envelope, the captain, second pilot, second coxswain and WT operator managed to clamber up and cling to the wreckage until rescued by a destroyer when daybreak dawned. Sadly the rest of the gallant crew drowned.

From this report it can be seen that airships, especially non-rigids, are susceptible to strong winds at ground level, Coastals and the larger North Seas presenting the greatest problems. It took 500 men to hold a North Sea class airship in turbulent conditions and even then it was a struggle. Torn hands and broken limbs were common. At least five deaths were recorded from ground-crew members who held on too long, falling from a great height while controlling a bucking airship. Airships (or aeroplanes of that period) could not operate in strong winds, but an airship with its duration of several hours, often found on its return to base, that the calm conditions of take-off no longer existed, hence the sometimes drastic conditions in which handling parties found themselves. The captain of a non-rigid always had another choice. In extreme cases he could 'rip' the envelope, causing instant deflation. A seam sewn along the top of the envelope led to a 'ripping-cord' adjacent to the coxswain. A stout pull – about 30 lb – broke this seam which then released the hydrogen into the air. Although the sudden loss of lift dropped the car(s), engine and crew violently onto mother earth, it seldom caused irreparable damage to the structure or serious wounds. However, this last-ditch operation was seldom used.

'Ripping' a non-rigid in extreme conditions is best illustrated by the occurrence at RNAS Longside on 21 September 1918. A recall signal was sent to her three airships flying that day, due to rising winds. The first to arrive was C.7 which landed safely into a 300-strong handling-party. Once in the lee of the shed and its windbreak their troubles began. The 45-mph wind caused back-eddies and down-draughts, tossing the airship around like a toy. Choosing his moment the captain ripped, and the deflated remains fell to the ground. Circling the field, two North Seas watched in trepidation. Another 200 men were summoned and eventually NS-9 nosed down into their hands. All went well until under the lee of the shed. NS-9 rose and fell 20 ft, almost out of control until her captain 'ripped'

Capt N. Grabowsky at the controls of his 'Zero' in 1918. The W/T Operator's head is seen in the front cockpit. The engineer (whose cockpit was behind the pilot, immediately in front of the Rolls-Royce 'Hawk' 75 hp engine) took the picture. It clearly shows the elevator wheel on the pilot's left, compass on the coaming behind the windshield, clock and other instruments. The Lewis-gun, stowed in its non-operational position (vertical), was never intended for defence purposes, but used frequently to shoot at floating mines, thus exploding them without the need to call on surface craft. (*Brian Turpin and Sydney Taylor*)

and she fell heavily but without serious damage to herself and crew. NS-10 approached in a similar manner and again, in the lee of her shed, was 'ripped'. By this time rain had set in and the crumpled remains of three fine airships lay spreadeagled in the mud. A sorry sight – but under normal conditions all would have been flying again within weeks. Owing to the Armistice on 11 November 1918, these three ships never did fly again. It is also the only occasion three airships were 'ripped' at the same time, on one station.

CHAPTER FIVE

British Rigid Airships 1917–19

After the battle of Jutland the Royal Navy laid plans for large rigid airships like the German Zeppelins. Germany had been building such craft since 1903 and gained immense experience. Nothing in the world could carry the weight and fly the distance of the 1916 Zeppelin. Naturally the Royal Navy had to start almost from scratch but due to a forced landing of the German Army Zeppelin Z.1V (the sixteenth Zeppelin built) at Lunéville, France, on 3 April 1913, sketches, measurements and photographs of this design were known. Vickers at Barrow had started a similar airship No. 9r in 1914 but because the Admiralty were concentrating on small, non-rigid, anti-submarine airships, work had been suspended in 1915: until Jutland. It was 27 December 1916 before this first British rigid airship to fly took to the air. Many modifications were required to make her even partially successful and it was not until April 1917 that she was accepted.

This sudden desire for large rigids after Jutland brought about a programme which was based upon an enlarged and modified No. 9r. These were the 23-class rigids. Six were built, with modifications being incorporated continuously. Vickers built the No. 23r, Beardmore at Inchinnan the No. 24r and Armstrong-Whitworth at Barlow built No. 25r. All flew trial flights between September and December 1917.

Crews for these rigids were taken from experienced Coastal-class airshipmen. Under Cdr Masterman, a Rigid Trials Flight was set up at Barrow and later at RNAS Howden. Airshipmen on these flights trained on the Parseval non-rigid airships (a German design,

Parseval No. 5, shortly after assembly at RNAS Howden where she was used by the Rigid Trials Flight to train crews for the forthcoming rigid airships. With her sister-ship, Parseval No. 6, she did yeoman work. The two Parsevals were not exact copies. They had different types of cars. (*JMB/GSL Collection*)

bought by the Admiralty and copied in three versions built by Vickers) which had certain flying characteristics similar to a rigid. Such was the expertise of these experienced airshipmen that when the British rigids started to arrive, there were crews available to fly them.

Let us briefly consider these early British rigid airships, 535 ft long, 53 ft in diameter with a volume of 942,000 cu ft of hydrogen to lift them. Built with four engines (later modified), they could lift approximately six tons. Of course, this did not include the crew, fuel and oil and armaments. When these were added, it left little to spare.

No. 24r, preparing for her trials flight on 28 October 1917, at Beardmore's airship works at Inchinnan. The rear car was dismantled and sent by rail to her war station of East Fortune. This reduction in weight enabled No. 24r to climb safely above the Scottish hills which separated the two places. (*Ces Mowthorpe Collection*)

But airshipmen were an ingenious lot. Brian Turpin, an authority upon the Royal Naval airship service relates:

No. 24r, built at Inchinnan by Beardmore had to cross the Scottish mountain range to get to her war station at East Fortune, on the East coast. Also it was imperative that No. 24 was cleared from the Inchinnan shed in order that work could be started on R.34, which was to be built in her 'space'. Unfortunately she was overweight by as much as three-quarters of a ton. The ship did not therefore meet its specification as far as useful lift was concerned. This increase in weight had largely come about through numerous small changes in the way the ship had been constructed during building, coupled with very little overall supervision of weight control by the manufacturers.

Drastic alterations were put in hand, to give the ship sufficient disposable lift to allow her to be flown to East Fortune where more permanent alterations could be made. To do this all the machinery, including the engine and swivelling propellers, were taken out of the after car. With the empty rear car remaining in place, the ship was flown across to East Fortune by following the Forth and Clyde canal, thus avoiding any mountains, on her three remaining engines. Dalmuir was passed at a height of 800 ft. Arriving safely at her war station she carried out her acceptance trials in this condition and was used for a short period as a (three-engined) training airship. It was hoped to fit a 33-class type wing car in place of the empty rear car but this did not happen. Eventually the original machinery was re-installed giving her back her fourth engine.

Speed was never an impressive item on early airships. A few months after the foregoing, No. 24r, now with her full complement of four engines was caught in a mild gale near the Bass Rock and despite full power, made no headway at all for several hours – some of the time actually moving astern.

A much modified sister-ship the R.27 (after No. 25r, the Royal Navy classified its rigid airships with a Capital R, instead of the No. —r, hence the next to be built was R.26 – rather than No. 26r) was the unfortunate victim of a well-intentioned plan at RNAS Howden.

An 'American contingent' had been training with the Royal Navy at Howden. Their task was to operate Zero non-rigids and then form an American flight, using Zeros bought from Britain. Training complete, they decided to make RNAS Howden a parting gift of another Zero. A used envelope and rudders were 'borrowed', likewise a spare car and engine. These they commenced to rig into a complete un-numbered Zero in the No. 1 shed. Petrol overflowed into the car during the filling of the fuel tank. It was not mopped up. When a wireless-rating fitting the wireless-set tested the same – a spark ignited the petrol fumes. This caused the airship's envelope to explode and set fire to the R.27 which was in the same shed. Another Zero was also destroyed in the conflagration. Oddly, the Parseval P.5, just inside the shed's door evaded destruction. The Parseval had a finely streamlined envelope and as it was at the 'upwind' end of the shed it was only scorched. Sadly an air mechanic on one of the sheds upper walkways was killed. The heat from the exploding hydrogen was so intense that it buckled the corrugated iron sheets forming the shed roof – more about this roof later!

We now have a smuggling story which could have come straight out of The *Boy's Own* Paper. The German firm of Schütte-Lanz were building rigid airships with a wooden framework, similar to the Zeppelins, which had an aluminium framework. Despite shortcomings, these were very efficient airships. A Schütte-Lanz works foreman was a Swiss national named Herr Herman Müller. During late 1915 Herr Müller stole a complete set of working drawings of their latest design from Schutte-Lanz, took them home to Switzerland, came by rail and ferry through France to England and sold the plans to the Royal Navy. Consequently the Royal Navy ordered Short Brothers, at their new Cardington works, to build two wooden airships from the smuggled plans (suitably modified). They were numbered R.31 and R.32. An important factor of these wooden airships was the patent *Kalt Leim* glue used to join the framework. Herr Müller had not got the formulae but knew the ingredients involved. Eventually in May 1916 British scientists developed a similar adhesive and work commenced.

R.31 was the first to fly in August 1918 but on her second flight (16 October), her upper fin collapsed. It was only thanks to a gallant working-party under Coxswain Cook (see p. 11 for Coxswain Cook's earlier adventure with the P.4), who climbed out onto the shattered framework, secured the collapsed structure to the hull while still in flight, near Reading, that she avoided destruction and was able to limp home to Cardington. Unfortunately, three weeks later Coxswain Cook was examining R.31's gasbags near the top of the hull when, overcome by escaping hydrogen, he fell down into the internal corridor. Severely injured, he was hospitalised for several months, during which time he was commissioned Lieutenant RN.

This was not the end of R.31's troubles. Repairs made, structures strengthened and trials completed, she set course for her war station

R.31 after landing safely at Cardington with a collapsed fin after her second trials flight on 16 October 1918. This is an excellent example of how the skill of airship crews saved airships in incidents which would have wrecked aeroplanes. Many accounts erroneously record that, upon landing, R.31's starboard elevator collapsed. As this picture shows, nothing of the sort occurred. The starboard elevator was damaged, but disconnected and secured, while the airship flew back using only her port elevator. (*Ces Mowthorpe Collection*)

at East Fortune under the command of Capt Sparling, via RNAS Howden, where an overnight stay took place. Departing next morning she was one hour into the flight when some of her wooden girders came apart. A disgruntled Capt Sparling managed to limp her back to Howden where she was hangared in No. 1 shed to await repairs. The date was 7 November 1918. Naturally, the Armistice celebrations delayed remedial action and consequently R.31 remained static in No. 1 shed for several months (as the war was now over, no one wanted airships). The reader will recall that it was No. 1 shed which suffered the damaged roof due to R.27's demise. The winter months of early 1919 were very wet. Rain poured in and onto the wooden R.31. When repairs were finally put under way it was discovered that the wooden structure was so warped through water damage that she was scrapped on the spot. There was a final twist to this story. R.31's wooden structure was sold to a local dealer who cut it up and sold it for firewood. Too late it was discovered that it had been pre-treated with a fireproof liquid and thus, refused to burn!

RNAS Howden was the scene of the loss of another fine British rigid: R.34, an almost identical copy to the Zeppelin L.33 which had been brought down virtually intact at Little Wigborough on 23 September 1916. Built by Beardmore at Inchinnan she was 643

The skeleton of R.31 in No.1 shed at RNAS Howden in March 1919, after she had been stripped of all salvageable material. It was in this condition that she was sold to a merchant near Howden, who dismantled and broke up her wooden remains for firewood. (*Ces Mowthorpe Collection*)

ft long, 79 ft in diameter and her nineteen gasbags contained 1,950,000 cu ft of hydrogen. Capable of lifting 26 tons, with 5–250 hp Sunbeam 'Maori' engines giving a top speed of 62 mph, she was, for her time, an efficient craft. On 2 July 1919, under the command of Maj G.H. Scott AFC, R.34 crossed the Atlantic bound for America. This was the first non-stop east–west journey and she was safely moored only when Maj Pritchard, OBE had parachuted down to take charge of the American mooring-crew. After spending several days in America, R.34 rose from Hazelhurst Field, Mineola and returned safely – the first aircraft to achieve the double crossing.

Let us consider the facts about this double crossing. One month earlier Alcock and Brown had made the first non-stop flight across the Atlantic, from west to east. No one must decry this splendid effort by two gallant airmen, in a modified Vickers 'Vimy' twin-engined aeroplane, without radio, in open cockpits. They flew from Newfoundland to Ireland in order to take the advantage of prevailing winds. R.34 however, almost in standard condition, flew from East Fortune to New York, against prevailing weather, carrying thirty men (plus one stowaway and the ship's cat), with full radio equipment. Refuelled and with the crew rested (?) she rose from her field and flew back again to Pulham. Admitted, her groundspeed was less than that of the Vickers 'Vimy' but in all other respects this airship flight portrayed the true beginnings of today's regular transatlantic schedules.

E.M. Maitland's book of this flight R.34 (Hodder & Stoughton, 1921) gives some idea of the navigational difficulties such a flight, in 1919 entailed. Maj Cooke, navigator explains:

Only three of seventeen astrological observations taken during the westbound flight could be made with reference to a clearly defined sea horizon; the remainder had to be estimated against a cloud horizon and were thus inherently inaccurate. Furthermore, with no information available on the surface pressure (air), the ship's altimeters were highly unreliable, so it was not possible to apply a height correction with any confidence. At one stage, by innovative use of his sextant to measure the actual height above sea level, Maj Cooke calculated that the ship's altimeters were nearly a 1,000 ft in error, this assessment being validated shortly afterwards when a sea level pressure reading was obtained by W/T from a nearby surface vessel. Cooke later estimated that in mid-Atlantic he had probably known the whereabouts of his craft to 'within fifty miles'.

The crew of the R.34 before lift-off for their successful double crossing of the Atlantic Ocean. This was the first double crossing, only a month after Alcock and Brown's first single crossing. Maj Scott is seated in the centre, in naval uniform. The ship's two mascots – Whoppsie and Mopsie – accompanied them over the Atlantic! (*Ces Mowthorpe Collection*)

The airshipmen of the RAF have never been given the credit they deserve for this achievement. It should, however, be understood that Germany had at least two airships and scores of superbly-trained airshipmen who could have accomplished this double crossing in 1918 – carrying also at least 2,000 lb of payload (passengers, freight or bombs). Returning from America, R.34 was overhauled and assigned to Howden in March 1920.

Departing there on the morning of 27 January 1921 under the command of Flt Lt Drew, a capable officer with a successful career ahead of him. Unfortunately Flt Lt Drew was unfamiliar with the Yorkshire coastline. Admiralty charts in use were not entirely up to date – despite the fact that eight trainee navigators were on board carrying out a navigational exercise. Far worse, the main radio apparatus developed a fault with its wave-meter, hence all messages sent were on an incorrect wavelength. Compounding these errors was the message, flashed by lamp as R.34 rose into the air, that her call-sign was 7VK. This should have read 7VF! Therefore all messages received by radio for 7VF were disregarded (R.32 was airborne at the same time and it was believed that 7VF was her call-sign). Eventually, using his standby spark radio, the operator contacted Flamborough Head wireless station who established contact with Howden, and all was revealed. It was now 1930 hrs and Drew assumed his position was 50 miles north, from Spurn.

Steering a course for base, R.34 battled against worsening weather as the night went on. Believing he had seen the Spurn light, Drew set course westwards for Howden. It was not the Spurn light. R.34 was soon over the North Yorkshire moors and with cloudbase decreasing height was reduced to 1,200 ft. About midnight her forward car scraped a hilltop near Guisborough, doing remarkably little damage but smashing the propellers on both front and rear gondolas. Ballast was released and R.34 lurched back into the air with only her two side-engine cars working. The strong westerly wind now blew the stricken airship back out into the North Sea but as daybreak came it lessened and by brilliant airmanship, Drew brought R.34 over base at 1600 hrs in failing light. Her exhausted crew's difficulties were not yet over. Despite the efforts of a 400-strong handling party, the rising and gusty wind prevented her entering her shed. Air Cdre Maitland, CO of RNAS Howden finally gave the order to abandon ship and R.34 was walked to the mooring rings further out in the airfield. Here she was secured by the three-wire system which at least held her down without endangering life. Sadly, the wind rose to gale force and the ship was constantly battered into the ground, doing severe damage to hull and gasbags. When morning broke it was obvious R.34 would never fly again. She was broken up over the next few days. A sad end to a gallant airship.

Recall R.31's fin breaking-off in mid-air (see p. 47)? On 1 April 1921, the latest British rigid R.36, civilianised by the addition of a passenger-car and bearing the registration G-FAAF was carrying Air Ministry officials and press correspondents when it met a similiar fate. In the words of her navigating officer, 'Tommy' Elmhirst:

Suddenly the ship went into a dive, both coxswains reporting they had lost control. Clawing my way to the engine telegraphs I rang 'Stop engines,' then stretched towards the water ballast tanks and let go half a ton of water – hoping this action would bring the bows level. Down the stairs came Scotty (Maj Scott – Captain) with a smile on his face saying, 'Tommy, what on earth have you been doing to the ship?' Maj Scott was imperturbable. He said, 'Get into the keel and stand at the top of the ladder where you can take orders from me. Distribute the crew at each of the cross-sections of the keel then move them a section at a time, forward or aft, as I order.' Thus by using a little power and moving the crew, control was regained, albeit only partially.

Both coxswains were sent to the top of the ship to report the damage while we drifted like a balloon, rudderless – between Bath and Bristol. The coxswains reported that both vertical and horizontal tail-surfaces had broken or buckled and that the whole tail might break off if too much power was applied. However, they thought they could disconnect the damaged elevator and rudder, secure them temporarily, then reconnect the lower rudder, rendering it usable. (For this the riggers were awarded Air Force Medals.) Finally Scotty turned to me and said, 'Tommy, find a replacement then get below and set me a course for home – I can only give you 30 knots.'

We reached Pulham at dusk and Maj Scott landed the ship perfectly using the crew in the keel as a 'climb and dive' control.

The civilian airship R.36 moored to the Pulham high mast in April 1921, before the incident described above by her Navigating Officer, 'Tommy' Elmhirst. The long passenger car, fitted below the huge rigid envelope, can be clearly seen. Also seen are her five engines – the forward two taken from a German Zeppelin (Maybachs), the other three being Sunbeam 'Cossacks'. Between the two port engine-cars is her civilian registration, G-FAAF. (*Ces Mowthorpe Collection*)

Just another example of the skill and ingenuity of airshipmen! A similar incident in an aeroplane would have meant certain disaster.

This book would not be complete without mentioning the gallant flight of R.33, the sister-ship to R.34, after she broke away from the Pulham mast in a gale on 17 April 1925. R.33 had been extensively reconditioned, given the civil registration G-FAAG and prepared for experiments connected with the proposed R.100 and R.101 civil airship programme. She moored to the Pulham mast after a pleasant flight under the command of Maj G.H. Scott on the 14 April.

The evening of 16 April saw R.33 majestically riding the Pulham high mast. An anchor-watch was aboard, performing normal 'harbour watch' duties. In the early hours of 17 April the relatively calm wind rose, with alarming suddenness, to gale force, gusting severely. R.33 however, rode the storm, head to wind, secured by her bow-coupling to the swivelling joint of the mast. Nevertheless, the crew was glad to be relieved at 0800 hrs by the next watch under Flt Lt R.S. Booth – an experienced captain.

Flt Lt Booth's first duty was to set his crew the task of examining the hull and equipment for any damage created by the stormy conditions. A rigger was sent out onto the mast-head with orders to check the security of the mast attachment. This man had a remarkable escape. With one foot on the airship's mooring cone and the other on the mast, he leant forward to inspect the coupling. At that moment a 50+ mph gust struck the airship. With a crack like a rifle-shot, the coupling parted, R.33 shooting away downwind. The unfortunate rigger threw himself backwards and fortunately, fell into the small circular platform surrounding the mast-head.

Meanwhile, on board R.33, Booth jettisoned all water ballast in an attempt to prevent the stricken ship colliding with the huge Pulham shed, immediately downwind. Slowly, so very slowly, the storm-driven airship lifted, missing the shed roof by what appeared to be inches. The first priority was to inspect the bows where the buckled nose-cone had penetrated and deflated the first gas-cell. Booth, accompanied by his very experienced coxswain, 'Sky' Hunt, clambered up to the upper gun platform, then, at great risk, crawled and clawed their way forward. The sight that met their eyes was far from encouraging. The fractured girders were swinging loosely and appearing at any moment likely to penetrate the second gas-cell. If that deflated, disaster was certain.

By this time, the engineers had got the Sunbeam 'Maori' engines started and still being driven backward through the sky, a modicum of stability was achieved. Because R.33 was being driven stern-first by the wind, the damaged nose was not subjected to undue wind forces. 'Sky' Hunt and a small team of volunteers scrambled up into the shattered bows and commenced securing the loose girders and flapping fabric of the shattered outer cover. In true seamanlike manner, eventually, the loose items were cut away and thrown overboard, while a jury-rigged framework was fastened forward of the critical second gas-cell. Finally, after three hours of dangerous, back-breaking work, battered by wind and drenched by the rain, 'Sky' Hunt and his gallant volunteers were safely back inside the ship.

Flt Lt Booth had established radio contact with the authorities as soon as he had obtained electrical power, his radio operator making reports every quarter of an hour. Naval vessels and lifeboats followed R.33 as she staggered backwards across the North Sea. Despite using her engines to retard her speed, the storm carried the airship down-wind much faster than the boats below could manage and soon she was out of sight and entirely alone. Gradually the wind abated and Booth was able to hold his ship steady and free from drift. His reported position was 45 miles north-east of IJmuiden, in Holland. By radio, he received offers of assistance from France, Holland and Germany. After due deliberation, these offers were declined.

Booth was faced with two problems. Would the jury-rigged bows hold and protect the second gas-cell when he got forward way on R.33? Furthermore, the heavy rain had so penetrated the outer cover and added weight that by now the ship was slowly losing what little height it already had. Fortunately, by late afternoon the rains ceased and gradually the wind abated. The crew had meanwhile thrown overboard every item that was movable and unnecessary, including fire extinguishers, life-jackets and spare clothing.

By 2000 hrs, blown slowly stern-first, R.33 crossed the Dutch coast and was actually several miles beyond IJmuiden. To protect the vulnerable jury-rigged nose, the airship was allowed to drift slowly stern first, to await calmer conditions. Gradually, as the outer cover dried off, Booth was able to report that he had gained height to nearly 8,000 ft. Pulham radioed the suggestion that he made for Cologne, where a landing-party of airshipmen would be waiting, and that the Dutch had landing-parties ready at two of their airfields. Pulham also kept the R.33 updated with forecast winds at all levels. Again Booth and his crew politely refused this most welcome international cooperation. Eventually, the wind dropped appreciably.

Slowly – approximate speed was 5 knots – the airship re-crossed the coast and gained the open sea. By now night had fallen and it was agreed that the ship would hold her position, just off the Dutch coast, until daylight.

At sunrise on 18 April, R.33 signalled Pulham 'Returning to England' and the long, slow homeward trek began. Carefully experimenting, Booth discovered that he could safely make 15 knots groundspeed. Anything greater and the damaged nose began to falter. Nine hours later R.31 appeared over her base at Pulham, where to scenes of tremendous jubilation, she was safely walked into her shed. The news of her plight had been broadcast over the BBC and hundreds of local Norfolk folk came to see her arrival. Pulham's CO, Maj Scott described the achievement of R.33 and her crew to be one of the greatest in airship history. 'Sky' Hunt was awarded the Air Force Medal and King George V later presented the entire crew with gold watches.

R.33's crew on this adventure were: Flt Lt Drew, Flt Sgt G.W. Hunt; the rest: G.E. Long, G. Watts, G. Bell, L. Moncrieff, C. Oliver, L. Rowe, R.Moyes, J. Walkinshaw, R. Dick, L. King, N. Mann, S. Scott, J. Scott, G. Potter, S. Keeley, W. Gent, J. Ramp, Z. Little.

A new nose section was designed and built, with extra strengthening added to withstand the stresses of mast-handling. This was fitted at Pulham and in October 1925, R.33 was airworthy again. She continued to provide a useful service to the National Physical

R.33 in the Pulham shed, with a horrendously buckled nose, after breaking away from the Pulham mast. Workers at the shed have stripped the torn outer cover from the broken framework. It is only by seeing damage such as this – which would have wrecked an aeroplane – that one can begin to understand why, in the 1920s, large rigid airships were often considered safer than aeroplanes. (*Ces Mowthorpe Collection*)

Laboratory until retired in November 1926 when after 735 hours flying time, her hull was found to be suffering from metal fatigue.

One cannot help but ponder about the inherent safety factor of airships (except of course the dreaded inflammable hydrogen/air mixture). This potential disaster and probable loss of twenty fine airshipmen was prevented by the prompt action of these experienced airshipmen. Even when R.101 crashed on the night of the 4/5 October 1930, although consumed by the exploding hydrogen, there were still six survivors and possibly, had R.101 used non-inflammable helium, all would have survived. Sad to relate, three survivors of the R.33 incident were lost in R.101: 'Sky' Hunt, S.E. Scott and S.T. Keeley. 'Sky' Hunt got clear of the initial impact but was seen to dash back into the burning wreckage in a valiant effort to rescue his pals.

At the end of the First World War, Great Britain had a number of rigid airships in the process of being built. All were virtually Zeppelin designs, copied from the Germans, who were themselves prevented from building any more airships by the terms of the peace treaty. This left only Britain with a rigid airship industry. When America wished to buy a rigid airship, to complement her home-built Zeppelin-based Shenandoah, still on the drawing-board, only Britain could deliver.

Short Bros were thrown out of their airship works at Cardington which then became the Royal Airship Works. Two rigids were under construction, R.37 and R.38 – R.37 was nearly complete, R.38 was composed basically of unassembled parts. The underlying thinking was that if Britain could successfully supply Zeppelin-type airships to America, a world-wide industry might be created. Vickers, basically responsible for all Britain's rigids, except R.31 and R.32 (which were Schutte-Lanz copies), was virtually ignored. The Royal Navy had a design team under Cdr Campbell (a qualified naval architect) which had monitored and modified Vickers' ships. Short Bros were financed and provided with the Cardington works in 1916, working with the Royal Navy and Cdr Campbell, to produce the Schutte-Lanz design. Hostilities ceased and in 1920, the Air Ministry reclaimed Cardington from Short Bros, renaming it The Royal Airship Works, appointing Campbell as Manager and Chief Designer. Now followed a change of policy. Work on all uncompleted rigids ceased. Except for R.38, it no longer had the original design but a completely new concept, which was expected to operate both at height as well as surface level, to be bought by the

American Navy. It was built by the Royal Airship Works at Cardington under chief designer Cdr Campbell, the Admiralty representative at Vickers throughout their building of Britain's wartime rigid airships. As such, he had acquired considerable experience and was directly responsible for Admiralty changes to the 23-class which produced R.27 and R.29, the Royal Navy's first 'operationally efficient' (just) airships.

Although he was a capable airshipman, Campbell, and the team he assembled, did not have the design and technical experience required for the task. Rigid airships were built by constructing large radial rings of suitable strength, then joining these rings together by longitudinal girders. Tail units, engine and control cars were fitted to this shell. The interior, except for a passageway along the keel was filled with the gas-cells between each radial ring. Lift from these gasbags was transmitted by netting affixed to the lower longitudinals. This simplification illustrates the basic requirements facing the design team.

The Zeppelin company and Vickers started by building relatively small rigids, with plenty of spare strength built in. Two factors then emerged. For operational purposes, airships grew bigger, and because of improved defences, they had to fly higher. The Zeppelin company built over 120 such airships and thus by sheer experience were able to dispense with much structural weight without imperilling performance. Also, the final wartime Zeppelins, the height-climbers, purposely lightly built, were flown by disciplined crews who never undertook violent manoeuvres in the denser air below 8,000 ft.

Vickers had Messrs Pratt and Barnes Wallis, two designers well aware of the fluid stresses at work around a large modern rigid airship. Barnes Wallis, specially worked out these stress factors during the building of his unique R.80. To illustrate the aerodynamic forces operating upon a large rigid, Barnes Wallis pointed out that, being lighter than the surrounding air, instead of flying straight through it like an aeroplane, an airship's nose oscillates around its flight path, even in still air. He called this 'curvilinear flight'.

Transmitted rearwards through the R.38's huge airframe (she was 699 ft long, 86 ft wide and 95 ft high) these forces were vastly greater than normal structural stresses. Sadly Campbell and his team were unaware of this particular point. Campbell built R.38 with a structural strength of four to one – an adequate margin which appeared to allow for manoeuvring and bad weather. After R.38

crashed into the River Humber, just missing the city of Kingston-upon-Hull, while returning to her shed at Howden, in Yorkshire, the Court of Inquiry found that when aerodynamic stresses were calculated, R.38's true strength was only one to one. This meant that in any stormy weather or violent manoeuvring she had no reserve strength.

Trial flights with R.38 had all been carried out in calm conditions. Even then mysterious breakages of girders had occurred. Repairs and reinforcments were undertaken. Her final testing flight was from Howden to Pulham, where she was to be moored to the mast, prior to handing over to her American crew for the transatlantic delivery flight. Arriving at Pulham on the evening of 23 August 1921, Capt Wann found the station shrouded in fog and orders were received to fly back to Howden overnight, and carry out further tests throughout the following day, before landing.

Quite what happened was never publicly ascertained. At 1747 GMT, R.38 was seen to turn sharply, then break up. Forty-nine souls were on board including the designer, most of his team and sixteen Americans. Five survived including Capt Wann.

The Court of Inquiry established the structural weaknesses mentioned above. But why, when information about airship stresses was already known, did Campbell remain ignorant of them? Cdr Campbell was not only designer of R.38, he also commanded the Royal Airship Works. His design brief was constantly altered and although much information on aerodynamic stresses was forwarded to Cardington from the National Physical Laboratory, he personally never got around to studying it. In the latter stages of designing and building R.38, Campbell had a tremendous workload which included trips to America and India. Thus he was unaware of vital information.

This book is about airshipmen and Cdr Campbell deserves a better status than is generally (with hindsight) awarded. He did much good work on airships, but finally, too much was demanded from him. Should any reader wish to find out more about the tragedy of R.38 I can fully recommend Tom Jamison's *Icarus over the Humber*, published by Lampada Press in 1988.

Readers must be aware from all the foregoing airship incidents that while certainly there were fatalities, the very nature of the airship, which floated, rather than being driven through the air like an aeroplane, made it a very resilient form of air transport. If the fire/explosion factor of hydrogen had been eliminated, by the use of a non-inflammable gas such as helium (of which very little existed in the 1920s) the fatalities would have been far fewer. Indeed, airshipmen were never unduly worried by the hydrogen that kept them aloft. Well-disciplined procedures ensured that the risk was minimal. Considering man-controlled flight was barely two decades of age, many professional airmen felt much safer in an airship than in an aeroplane.

The lifting agent of most airships was hydrogen but few people realise what huge quantities were consumed, especially at the large rigid stations. While not true 'airshipmen', without the operators of hydrogen gas plants, airships could not have flown. As we shall see, this task was not without inherent danger.

By 1916, the Royal Navy had a large number of portable gas plants, using the silicol principle, distributed to war stations. Gas produced was then stored in either cylinders or small gasometers. With the coming of the large non-rigids and rigid airships, these were replaced or assisted by fixed plants capable of making up to 10,000 cu ft per hour. True to its principles, the Navy distributed an *Admiralty Hydrogen Manual* covering all aspects of silicol plants. This was necessary because producing hydrogen from silicol was subject to risk.

At RNAS Pulham in Norfolk, on 14 February 1917 the silicon gas-plant blew up. Lt Wildmass was blown through the shed wall and killed immediately. The hydrogen officer, Lt Mitten, was covered in caustic soda and seriously injured. Several civilians and two more officers suffered severe burns.

A new plant was built using a less dangerous method of steam and iron which produced 14,000 cu ft per hour. These steam/iron plants became standard although experiments were carried out with breaking water into hydrogen and oxygen, using an electrolytic process.

The transatlantic flight in 1924 of LZ-126 (*Los Angeles*) and later in 1928, the LZ-127 (*Graf Zeppelin*) caused many minds in this country to believe that the only sound method of linking the (then) British empire by air, was a similar British airship. Certainly there was a nucleus of highly skilled airshipmen capable of carrying out such flights.

Two airships, larger than any other to date, were designed and built: R.100 by a subsidiary of Vickers, called the Airship Guarantee Company, and R.101 by the reorganised Royal Airship Works at Cardington. Much has been written about these two British giants, especially R.101. As this is a book about airshipmen, fair comment must be made regarding certain facts.

During the First World War, the Admiralty was heavily dependent upon Vickers for warships, submarines, airships and aeroplanes. Indeed, Vickers was vital to the wartime Royal Navy. Being a civilian and therefore profit-making company, often meant that there were other considerations, as well as simple service requirements. Civilian designers in all departments clashed with their Royal Navy counterparts on numerous occasions. Airships were a case in point. Having designed and built the original No. 9 and 23-class, all be it to Admiralty specifications, Vickers were supervised by a team under construction Cdr C.I.R. Campbell, a naval architect. By 1916, the Admiralty began to design and modify designs, without consulting Vickers. Pratt and Barnes Wallis with their design teams at Vickers were constantly frustrated. Yet Vickers' superiority was established beyond logical doubt by Barnes Wallis's remarkable R.80, perhaps the most efficient airship Britain ever possessed.

When hostilities ceased, all service rigid airship design was centred at the newly established Government Royal Airship Works at Cardington (formerly Short Bros) under the direction of Cdr C.I.R. Campbell. But when the R.38 broke up in 1921 with the loss of Campbell and most of his team all airship work in Britain ceased.

By 1924 rigid airships were again to the fore with the proposed Empire route, England–India. Parliament sanctioned a socialist/ capitalist scheme where two giant airships would pioneer air routes throughout the (then) British Empire. From the start, this competitive building scheme split airshipmen into two camps, Vickers (capitalist) versus the rest (Royal Airship Works). Sadly, as so often happens, politics came into the picture. In 1925 work commenced on R.100, the 'capitalist' ship, to be built at the old RNAS Howden large No. 2 shed. The 'socialist' ship, R.101, was to be built by the government at the Royal Airship Works, Cardington.

Both R.100 and R.101 were over 700 ft long, with a gas capacity of 5,000,000 cu ft of hydrogen. Bearing in mind the R.38 disaster, extreme care was taken to build strong airworthy airframes. Tests and experiments were carried out at both Cardington and the National Physical Laboratory towards this end.

There the similarity ended. Barnes Wallis, heading the Vickers contingent at Howden built R.100 exactly to his original design. Apart from changing the engines from the proposed diesel to petrol, because no suitable diesel engines were available, Barnes Wallis stuck to his original plans. The result was a very practical, long-range airship which satisfactorily made eight proving flights around

Airship at St Huberts,
Montreal, Canada, August 1930.
(*Ces Mowthorpe Collection*)

Britain; and then, on 29 July 1930, successfully carried out a double crossing of the Atlantic, mooring to the Montreal mast and making a sightseeing trip around Niagara Falls, prior to her return flight.

Sadly R.101 was a different story. From the beginning, being a government ship, she was exposed to considerable publicity. Great expectations were predicted. Innumerable alterations were ordered but as in the case of R.100, no suitable diesel engines were (then) available. Great play had been made by both the government and the national press that R.101 would have considerably less fire risk, especially in the tropics, because it used diesel fuel. Hence the designers felt unable to change to petrol motors. They were stuck with very heavy diesels which never developed anything like their stipulated power. The crunch came when on her trial flight, R.100 only had a lifting capacity of 35 tons instead of the proposed 55 (even R.100 was slightly heavy, her useful lift being 54 tons).

Drastic modifications were undertaken, including adding an extra bay and gas-cell amidships (increasing her total length to 777 ft, 44 ft longer than her initial design). A total of eleven trial flights, all in calm conditions, were made around Britain and finally, she set off to India on the evening of 4 October 1930 in the face of worsening weather. Crossing the Beauvais ridge in northern France she fell to earth and a few seconds later exploded into flames with the loss of forty-eight brave souls, including her designer and several key members of his team. This was the world's worst air disaster of 1930.

The above paragraphs greatly over-simplify the lives of these two British airships and the traumas which their airshipmen underwent. Excellent details of R.100 are contained in Capt George Meager's book *My Airship Flights* (published in 1970 by William Kimber). The story of R.101 can be found in Sir Peter Masefield's *To Ride the Storm* (published in 1982 by William Kimber) and *The Millionth Chance* by James Leasor (published in 1957 by Hamish Hamilton).

R.101 incorporated many innovative new features, all apparently good. Due to various pressures from the media she was built up as a wonder ship. Time prevented remedies being carried out. The political necessity of proving herself, after R.100's triumphant double Atlantic crossing, drove her crew to take off under weather conditions which were quite unsuitable. The result was disaster.

Once again Britain cancelled all airship development immediately. Within months R.100 was reduced to scrap in her Cardington shed. One often gets the opinion that R.100 was a huge success and R.101 a ghastly mistake. This is not a correct evaluation. R.100 had her faults and R.101 her good points. All accidents are preventable but sometimes, tragedies such as the sinking of the RMS *Titanic*, the loss of HMS *Hood* and the collapse of the Tay Bridge appear to be brought about by forces beyond the human ken. R.101 comes into this category.

What is relevant is that R.38, R.100 and R.101 were flown by some of the world's finest airshipmen. The design teams, likewise, were of high calibre. Both R.38 and R.101 were, for their time, very advanced designs. If political pressure had not prevented proper trials, R.101, with her sister-ship R.100, may have created a true Empire air service. The aeroplane would, in the end, have taken over but with non-inflammable helium becoming available, the airship could have pioneered an earlier era of luxury air travel.

Germany had her Count Zeppelin, Dr Durr and Professor Schutte. In Britain there was one man who could be called their equal. That man was Barnes Neville Wallis – later Sir Barnes Wallis. Indentured as an engineer to the Thames Engineering Company he moved on and became a draughtsman to John Samuel White of Cowes. Here he became friendly with another draughtsman H.B. Pratt, a former employee of Vickers at Barrow and a member of the design team of the ill-fated HMA No. 1r (nicknamed *Mayfly*).

When Vickers received an order for HMA No. 9r in September 1913 they recalled Pratt, who took Wallis with him. This was the

Barnes Wallis – later Sir Barnes Wallis – in the early 1950s. The paintings on the wall behind show his first rigid aurship, No. 9r (on the right), and the nose of his last rigid airship, R.100 (on the left). (*Ces Mowthorpe Collection*)

start of Wallis's remarkable career in airships. After many interruptions the No. 9r flew, more or less successfully, in 1917 and was the basis for the first British rigids Nos 23–25r and R.26, R.27 and R.29. Some of these were sub-contracted but Pratt and Wallis were primarily the designers.

Then, because Vickers had no shed large enough to build the later rigids, Wallis was given a completely free hand to design the R.80, within the confines of the existing shed at Barrow-in-Furness. Unfortunately, the Armistice, political and labour delays, prevented her commissioning until January 1921 but when she eventually took to the skies, R.80 proved to be the most efficient British rigid airship to date. Barnes Wallis was not only an engineer, he had an artist's eye. R.80 was beautifully proportioned and every part of her streamlined. Her interior controls, cables, valves, etc., were all colour-coded. Sadly, due to the running down of all services and the tragedy of the R.38, R.80 was broken up after only 90-hrs flying-time.

In 1924 Vickers formed a subsidiary, the Airship Guarantee Company, to build a 5,000,000-cu ft airship in competition with the newly-formed Royal Airship Works government-funded R.101. Barnes Wallis became the chief designer for this airship, the privately-built R.100.

From its inception, R.100 was the brainchild of Barnes Wallis. He personally worked out each individual problem and stress. With innovative engineering he produced a most successful airship which met all her specifications. Again using his artist's eye, Barnes Wallis designed her with beautiful symmetry. Her lines, like the R.80's, were the last word in streamlining. R.100 was a rigid airship but unlike her predecessors she owed little to Zeppelin practice.

Her return flight to Canada in July 1930 proved her strength and duration beyond doubt. Off the American coast she was struck by a squall of terrific force, similar to that which had broken the American rigid ZR-1 *Shenandoah* into three pieces. Despite superficial damage, R.100 flew on. Had disaster not befallen the R.101 at Beauvais a few months later, there is little doubt that R.100, like her predecessor No. 9r, would have been the first of many similar airships.

Following in the steps of the German Count Zeppelin, Barnes Wallis transferred his allegiance to aeroplanes and although still in a consultant capacity during the latter stage of building and flying R.100, he was by that time personally and heavily involved in designing the Vickers Wellesley bomber, the first aeroplane to be built on the geodetic principle.

This geodetic principle was derived from Barnes Wallis's ingenious netting system which transmitted the lift from her gas-cells to her rigid framework. Although Barnes Wallis pioneered this geodetic netting, it is interesting to note that Dr Parseval had employed a basically similar system for the suspension of the gondolas in his large non-rigids, patented as the Parseval tangential wiring. Professor Schutte also based the wooden framework of his first Schutte-Lanz airship upon a similar principle.

One of the greatest dangers an airship faces, is its vulnerability when being handled on the ground in strong winds. This is a particularly hazardous procedure when entering a shed. Wind eddies over the building can make an airship, which is lighter-than-air, leap around alarmingly. The larger the airship, the greater the problem. Many airshipmen felt this problem could be overcome by mooring airships to masts. Thus secured, they could ride out any storm, swinging head to wind, as a ship does at anchor. Ironically, the German Zeppelin company had investigated this idea and discounted it – preferring to use rotating sheds. While rotating sheds were a brilliant conception, they proved too complicated and expensive to build extensively. Consequently many flying days were lost to them in the First World War due to Zeppelins being confined to their static sheds in quite moderate winds.

By 1918, RNAS Pulham, at this period an experimental as well as an operational station, was looking into the possibilities of mooring-masts. Many small masts were erected, old SS non-rigids being used to solve the various problems. Later that year, up to four airships could be seen at any one time, permanantly moored for weeks on end, evaluating different systems. Vickers at Walney Island independently commenced experimenting. (Remember, it was Vickers who devised the simple mooring-mast for the HMA No. 1 (*Mayfly*) in 1911.)

In 1919, Pulham finally erected a 'high mast', especially for mooring rigid airships, together with a practical mooring method. This basically meant that the airship flew to the vicinity of the mast dropping a line. This line was connected to line from the mast, laid out across the airfield, then the airship was winched in until a special fitting in the nose connected and locked with a mating piece at the mast-top. There, the ship rotated with the wind, secure. Fuel and gas supplies all led to this mast-top. Crews could climb (at Pulham) a spiral staircase to a top platform which connected to the moored airship by means of a companion-way. It was a highly refined version of this Pulham mast which was erected at Cardington, Montreal and Ismailia for the proposed Empire routes which the ill-fated R.101 and her sister-ship R.100 were to have used.

The Ismailia mooring-mast, identical with the Cardington mast. Together with the mast at Karachi, these three were the staging-posts for the England–India Empire Airship route. Note the 60,000-gallon water tank alongside. This was meant to fill the water ballast tanks of the rigid airships as they staged through. Gas and fuel supplies would have been available. Never used, together with the airship-shed at the Karachi terminus, all were subsequently scrapped. (*Ces Mowthorpe Collection*)

The Pulham mast used a traction-engine's winch, hired from a local firm, for pulling the rigids to the mast-head. Cardington, Montreal and Ismailia all had purpose-built steam winches and lifts for personnel.

Pulham was the scene of many experiments with airships during the period 1919–21. As mentioned earlier, at RNAS Kingsnorth in 1915, Cdr N. Usborne RN, had suspended an aeroplane beneath an airship's envelope (the AP-1) in a sadly, fatal attempt to defeat the German Zeppelins. This idea of carrying an aeroplane aloft beneath an airship, then releasing it to fly away, was expanded further at Pulham.

Major Ivo Little, RAF, and Lt Edward Crook, RAF (both experienced airship captains) designed a release-gear (known as the 'Little-Crook anchoring-gear') for dropping a Sopwith Camel from the British Rigid R.23. The aeroplane was suspended beneath No. 8 frame, between the front and amidships gondolas. During the morning of 5 November 1918 (after many previous static tests), the Camel was winched up into position while on the ground, R.23 then took off and flew around the Pulham station. The Camel was not occupied, this test being purely to test the release and the reaction of the aeroplane (and airship) afterwards. All went well, the Camel, upon release, assumed its natural gliding attitude and made a crash landing below. The experiment was deemed successful and two volunteers were accepted for full piloted trials.

On 6 November 1918, Lt R.E. Keys, RAF, climbed into the cockpit of another Sopwith Camel, the engine was started prior to flight and again R.23 took off from Pulham. When a suitable height was reached, Lt Keyes operated the release mechanism and again the little aeroplane dropped away from her mother-craft.

The captain of R.23 on both these epic experiments was Maj I.C. Little, co-inventor of the release system. His official report to the CO of RAF Pulham, dated 14 November 1918 is worth quoting:

The unpiloted Sopwith Camel No. N6814, suspended beneath No. 23r, prior to being dropped using the 'Little-Crook anchoring gear', on 3 October 1918, near RAF Pulham. (*Ces Mowthorpe Collection*)

In accordance with instructions on Wed. 6 November 1918.

1400 hrs   R.23 left shed with aeroplane slung beneath. Lt Keyes (?) in the pilot's seat.

1500 hrs   Aeroplane engine was started.

1507 hrs   Ship left ground and rose steadily to 3,000 ft.

1525 hrs   Proceeded course 27 degrees into wind, air speed 30 mph.

1528 hrs   Slipped aeroplane. The machine dropped away from the ship for about 12 ft and then went into a glide. The machine appeared to be under control two seconds from slipping. The airship rose 200 ft after slipping before she could be checked.

1600 hrs   Ballasted up for landing.

1617 hrs   Landed.

Remarks: Tail support was hauled-up five minutes before slipping. Slip worked perfectly. No jar was felt in the ship when aeroplane was released.

Senior airshipmen at Pulham were not only concerned with releasing fighter aeroplanes to defend the mother airship. Thoughts about engine-cars and gondolas fitted with wings and tail-units, which could be 'slipped' if required were under consideration. Maj Boothby, CO of RAF Pulham proposed: 'That the centre car of R.23 be replaced by a large aeroplane, constituting a unit which will normally contribute to the propulsive power of the airship but which could be released if it was required to attain maximum possible altitude or if the ship was seriously heavy when required to land.'

It is a tribute to all airshipmen that such experiments were undertaken in these comparatively early days of flight. Only a large rigid airship could have accomplished such tasks. Later, in 1921, the RAF experimented with 'an airship and overhead wire landing gear for small craft' but nothing further came of this effort to retrieve aeroplanes.

The R.38 disaster in 1921 brought the RAF's work with airships to a sudden halt. They were scrapped and the crews either discharged or incorporated into aeroplane squadrons. All that is, except the R.33. This rigid had been passed over to the civilian authorities and given the registration G-FAAB, while still based at Pulham, and was subsequently placed in store there. When Ramsay Macdonald's Labour Government initiated an Airship Research Policy in 1924, R.33 was extensively overhauled and recommissioned.

Dropping and retrieving aeroplanes from airships came under this research policy and at that time the RAF possessed two De Havilland 'Humming Birds' (Nos J.7325/6), ultra-light aeroplanes. A special

De Havilland DH.53 Humming Bird L7325 (26-hp Blackburne Tomtit engine), suspended beneath R.33 on 15 October 1925, with Sqn Ldr Rollo de Haga Haig in the cockpit. After release the pilot failed to re-engage with the airship. The propeller broke through, catching the release-gear, and a successful forced landing was made. After being fitted with a more powerful engine, a second DH.53 was used and Sqn Ldr de Haga Haig successfully re-engaged with the airship on 4 December 1925. (*Ces Mowthorpe Collection*)

'hook and suspension' system was devised. The 'hook' was a strong braced contraption which incorporated a propeller guard attached to the aeroplane. The 'suspension' incorporated a large 'loop' (into which the 'hook' was flown) plus further bracings, fastened below the R.33.

The well-known (and well-liked) Farnborough test-pilot, Sqn Ldr R.A. de Haga Haig, volunteered to fly the 'Humming Bird'. Static tests first established the feasibility of the apparatus and on 15 October 1925, R.33 ascended from Pulham. Sqn Ldr de Haga Haig dropped away successfully but failed after several attempts, to re-engage with the airship. The under-powered light aeroplane was unable to manoeuvre in the slipstream of the airship. Modifications, including a more powerful engine were made and a further test carried out later that month. This was also a failure. On 4 December, de Haga Haig finally succeeded. He later wrote in the journal *Aviation*:

> We examined all available data with regard to attaching a machine to an airship and maintaining contact between the two aircraft, which had been carried out during the war in England and later in the United States. (America had successfully flown off and retrieved a Sperry monoplane to a small non-rigid in 1924.) From this data it

became evident that very little was known of the airflow in the vicinity of a large airship in flight, and that an experiment of this sort, to be really satisfactory, would mean providing a single hook on the aeroplane, under the control of the pilot, for hooking on a considerable distance below the airship. Furthermore, some buffer arrangement was necessary to prevent the plane damaging either itself or the airship when actually attached, and some means had to be adopted for checking the sway of the machine when hauling up.

Sqn Ldr de Haga Haig also held the belief that the buffeting and turbulence he experienced from the combined airflows of plane and ship while 'hooking-on', could seriously strain the airships structure if a much heavier aircraft than the ultra-light 'Humming Bird' was used. Thus although a further successful dropping experiment was carried out with R.33 in October 1926 using two Gloster Grebe fighters (piloted by Flg Off Mackenzie-Richards, RAF, and Flg Off Ragg, RAF) attached by a modified 'Little-Crook anchoring-gear', retrieval was never considered.

German airshipmen had experimently dropped an aeroplane from an airship. In January 1918 an 'Albatross' fighter was taken aloft by a training airship L.35 and successfully launched. No attempt was made to re-attach the aeroplane to the airship and subsequently interest waned.

However on the 11 March 1937, Ernst Udet, the well-known German pilot, carried out a number of experiments with the LZ.129 *Hindenburg* while flying a Focke-Wulf 44 light biplane. He successfully 'hooked-on' to the airship, launched again and re-attached. The apparatus used was similar to that which was fitted to the R.33 and used by Sqn Ldr de Haga Haig in 1925. Nothing further came of this experiment as all airships were grounded after the *Hindenburg* disaster at Lakehurst on 7 May 1937.

As we shall see later, the American Navy brought the idea of a 'flying aircraft-carrier' to fruition with their super-rigids, *Akron* and *Macon* during the 1930s.

While Great Britain opted out of the airship scene after the R.101 disaster in 1930, the mast ideas, pioneered by Vickers, Capt Scott and Cdr Masterman – to name only a few – were used over the next twenty years by the US Navy in their extensive airship programmes.

Mechanical ground handling of airships was pioneered at Pulham. In 1918 a specially-built manoeuvrable caterpillar tractor was used for taking airships onto the airfield, aided by manpower. Later still, in 1919 an ex-army tank was 'borrowed'. On the rear of this tank was built a 20-foot mooring-mast. The large rigids could then be secured and handled better while on the ground. Some idea of the lifting-power of a rigid airship in gusty conditions is better understood when it is recalled that on several occasions the ex-army tank was lifted off the ground in gusts! All these innovative ideas were the result of much trial and error by airshipmen as they endeavoured to carry out their duties in the most efficient manner possible – despite being constrained by lack of funds.

CHAPTER SIX

German Airshipmen

G ermany is the true home of airships. Count Zeppelin's influence upon the design of the large rigid is undisputed. His company built and flew 130 rigid airships – mostly with great success. In wartime, Zeppelins formed an airborne weapons system which continued to influence all air forces long after the airship itself disappeared. Both before and after the First World War, Zeppelins proved themselves as passenger carriers when other aircraft had neither the range or carrying-power. The Schutte-Lanz firm, independent of the Zeppelin company built eighteen rigids to their own, similar, design.

This success story was bought at the expense of many airshipmen during the First World War because of the vulnerability of hydrogen-filled gasbags against increasingly efficient aeroplanes armed with exploding incendiary ammunition. This one fact apart, the German Zeppelin had an enviable record of passenger-carrying safety despite picturesque incidents which would have proved fatal in an ordinary aircraft.

Count Zeppelin was without doubt the prime mover of the Zeppelin rigid airship, but it was a little-known engineer, engaged by the Count as an ordinary working engineer on the first Zeppelin, whose practical and methodical approach to the mechanics of rigid airship construction, brought about their successes. Ludwig Durr (later Dr Ludwig Durr) stepped in when the designer of LZ-1, Engineer Kubler, refused to fly in his brainchild. Retained later by Count Zeppelin, it was Durr who provided the practical applications of the Count's designs. Described by a colleague: 'A typical Swabian, ill at ease when dealing with outsiders, like a hermit. Never travels, with narrow views. Believes in German theory of absolute secrecy about his work, builds just about as he pleases and is a very difficult man to deal with.'

Yet through his own efforts – he built a wind-tunnel at his own expense during the early days – by trial and error, plus the Count's enthusiasm, he perfected, for its day, the near-perfect flying machine. He was also an experienced airship pilot. Count Zeppelin died after a short illness in March 1917. During the last eighteen months of his life, his interest in the rigid airship had waned and his remaining energies were directed towards extra-large aeroplanes such as the Staaken Giant and the huge Dornier flying-boat, in both of which he held financial interests. Meanwhile, it was left mainly to Ludwig Durr to carry out the vastly improved development of the rigid airship. While Count Zeppelin and Dr Eckener became household names, the quiet man who made it all possible was Dr Ludwig Durr.

A commercial off-shoot of the Zeppelin company, Deutsche Luftschiffahrts AG (DELAG), was formed in May 1909 and took delivery of the LZ-7 named *Deutschland* in July 1910. This was a new ship with three engines and a saloon built into the keel capable of carrying twenty-four passengers. Note the year – 1910. It was only in 1903 that the Wright brothers had made the first aeroplane flight! Few aircraft other than an airship could have carried more than two people, or stayed in the air for more than a few minutes. Yet DELAG was confident of becoming a commercial proposition.

Under command of Capt Kahlenberg, an experienced pilot from the Prussian Airship Battalion, the *Deutschland* prepared for a 3-hour cruise carrying twenty-three journalists on what today would be called a PR exercise. Things went wrong. Despite a maximum speed of 37 mph, the airship was blown downwind and was unable to regain her base against the rising wind. An engine failed and heavy with rain the *Deutschland* wallowed around the sky for nine hours. Over the Wallendorf forest the captain decided on a forced landing – among the tree-tops. This was carried out successfully and although a complete wreck the ill-fated ship did not catch fire. The only casualty was a broken leg. Capt Kahlenburg was dismissed from DELAG.

Following the above incident, an existing Zeppelin was modified to carry twelve passengers and with Dr Hugo Eckener as pilot carried out thirty-four passenger flights in August and September.

A replacement for the above *Deutschland* (also named *Deutschland*), was completed, taken over by Eckener and flown from a base at Düsseldorf. After twenty-four successful passenger flights, Dr Eckener had this *ersatz Deutschland* taken from the shed in marginal weather conditions on 16 May 1911. Despite the efforts of 300 men,

This postcard shows the *Ersatz Deutschland* pinioned onto the end of her shed on 16 May 1911. Dr Eckener never again allowed himself to be persuaded to fly when weather conditions were doubtful. By amazing good luck no casualties ensued, but the airship was a write-off. It was this incident that made Eckener realise the importance of intensive training, thus establishing a firm foundation for all future Zeppelin operations. (*Peter Wright via Ces Mowthorpe Collection*)

control was lost and the airship ended up impaled on the shed, a complete wreck. Fortunately no lives were lost. Never again did Dr Eckener allow his judgement to be swayed by economic possibilities, going on to become the greatest airship pilot of all times.

Dr Eckener realised that for successful airship operations, much training was required. During the winter of 1910–11 both ground and aircrews undertook an extensive programme covering ground handling, effects of temperature changes, gas purity etc. Also the unreliable Daimler engines were to be replaced on all future ships with the specially-designed Maybach 145-hp motors. Basing operations at Baden-Oos (Baden-Baden) where the shed was built in a sheltered valley, Dr Eckener had special 'docking-rails' laid, a hundred yards out into the field from the shed doors. By securing the airship to trolleys on these rails, disasters similar to that which destroyed the second *Deutschland* were greatly minimised.

The tenth Zeppelin built, slightly smaller than the *Deutschland* was accepted by DELAG in July 1911 and given the name *Schwaben*. This airship really gave birth to the passenger-carrying Zeppelin fleet. Carrying twenty-four fare-paying passengers she made up to three local flights a day, of three hours' duration, throughout the summer. Flights to Frankfurt and Düsseldorf took place if the weather was suitable and one excursion to Berlin was undertaken. Fares varied between 150 and 600 marks. To view their beloved country from a Zeppelin became a popular pastime for those fortunate enough to afford such luxuries.

Bearing in mind that in 1911 flight of any kind was considered to be a somewhat risky procedure, DELAG had nothing to offer except the novelty. Hence their brochure, which went to great lengths extolling the safety of their airships. This is an extract from, 'Passagier-Fahrten Mit Zeppelin-Luftschiffen, 1911':

It is so constructed as an integral part of the ship that the longitudial framing of the airship at the same time forms the framing of the cabin. It is further braced so securely in position by twelve pairs of steel cables that it will hang immovable from them. It is so constructed as an integral part of the ship that even if, through some unlikely accident, a couple of struts should bend or break. All metal parts of the cabin frame are covered on the inside with mahogany while the ceiling and walls consist of mahogany plywood. Rich mother-of-pearl inlays on the ceilings beams and pillars cause the cabin to appear as an extraordinary comfortable and elegant room. The floor, which is constructed with absolute safety of five-layered plywood, is covered with carpet. Large sliding windows permit an unhindered view in all directions. The light wicker-work furniture provides comfortable seating.

A chef accompanied each flight, working from a miniscule kitchen fitted at the end of the cabin. Cold meals were available of cavier, pâté de foie gras, ham and capon. Fine wines from the Moselle, Rhine, Bordeaux and Champagne added to the luxury. These of course were extra to the cost of the flight.

For the 1912 season, after the winter lay up, another larger Zeppelin, L.11, *Victoria Louise* began operations from Frankfurt and proved a great success. Sadly, *Schwaben* was destroyed by fire on the ground at Düsseldorf after an excursion flight. The cause was discovered to have been static electricity, which had built up while in flight and caused a spark when two of the rubberised gas-cells rubbed together, igniting hydrogen which was escaping through the valves. The conflagration consumed the ship. From then on, all later Zeppelins used gas-cells of non-rubberised material. (Except perhaps the *Hindenburg*. Built in 1936, this magnificent airship was planned to be inflated with the non-inflammable gas helium. America refused to export this gas so the normal hydrogen was substituted. Sadly, it is believed by the author that the gas-cells were not changed and possibly contributed to *Hindenburg's* tragic demise at Lakehurst, New Jersey in May 1937.)

Thankfully a sister-ship to *Victoria Louise*, the L.13 *Hansa* had just been completed which carried out the ill-fated *Schwaben's* flights. A double hangar was constructed at Hamburg, and further sheds at Düsseldorf, Potsdam, Leipzig and Gotha. Fields became available at Stuttgart, Munich, Dresden, Braunschweig and Liegnitz. May 1913 saw the addition of a further airship L.17 *Sachsen*. Together, this small fleet of Zeppelins flew through the skies of southern Germany until the outbreak of the First World War in August 1914. Altogether DELAG flew 1,588 passenger flights carrying 10,197 fare-paying passengers, all in comparative luxury and safety. Although never a scheduled airline, DELAG laid the foundations for what, today, every airline passenger takes for granted – and all before the First World War. No passengers or crewmen lost their lives.

The German forces, Army and Navy, had both cast envious glances at Count Zeppelin's rigid airships. There was in existence a Prussian Airship Battalion with considerable experience on small non-rigids. Despite some resistance from the traditional generals and admirals, both forces bought Zeppelins before the outbreak of the First World War. Crews were trained by the successful civil operators DELAG, thus ensuring some operational experience before transferring back to

From a poster advertising 'Passenger Flights with Zeppelin Airships 1913'. (*Ces Mowthorpe Collection*)

the military arm. Sadly, through mismanagement and grossly exaggerated expectations, most of these early military airships met with disaster. The cost in both monetary and human terms was considerable. However, the German people were so impressed by the DELAG operations that eventually the rigid airship arm was developed into both an efficent reconnaissance and offensive weapon. This is not a war book, but as the rigid airship crews of Germany were the largest operators of these giant craft, certain extracts from wartime operations are necessary if we are to present a genuine picture of pioneering airshipmen.

Even the Zeppelins used during 1914, very early models, could carry 4,000 lb of bombs for 'short' raids into France, spherical bombs of 110 lb, 220 lb and 330 lb being carried initially. Naturally bomb aimers had to see the target – not always possible on a cloudy night. Captain of the Army airship Z.X11, Oblt z S Lehman and his fellow officer von Gemmingen devised a 'sub-cloud car' (*Spahkorb*) that was winched down below their airship, complete with an observer who remained in touch with the mother-craft via telephone. Thus while Z.X11 flew above cloud, she was directed to the target by the sub-cloud car observer. Several designs were tested and the final one fitted to a number of early Army Zeppelins. There was only one successful raid using the 'sub-cloud car' – on Calais, in early 1915. It was a complete surprise to the citizens of Calais, the airship drifting

This is the sub-cloud car found in a field in the Home counties after the Zeppelin raid on the night of 2/3 September 1916. It had been jettisoned, together with its winch. Apparently it had 'run away' while being prepared for launching because a crow-bar was found jammed in the winch gears. Contrary to many rumours, no body was found inside. The Zeppelin concerned was the Army Airship LZ.90. (*Imperial War Museum*)

silently on one throttled-back motor while dropping 6,000 lb of bombs on the town. The French military thought they were being shelled by a long-range gun! However, the car and its winch weighed half a ton, so it was soon done away with in favour of increased bomb-load. Despite the apparent perils of the 'sub-cloud car', there was no shortage of volunteers for observers – they were allowed to smoke while below the airship – a privilege normally forbidden among airship crews!

These early Zeppelins carried a crew of nineteen, a powerful radio cabin and up to eight heavy machine-guns for defence. Three of these machine-guns were situated on an exposed open platform on the top of the hull above the nose, manned by two brave gunners who had to fight off aircraft while standing in a 45-mph slipstream, totally exposed. They were fastened to the hull by strong cables. Imagine their feelings when attacked. The howling slipstream, a vertical rising of 1,500 ft per minute as ballast was dropped to gain height, then the order from the captain to stop shooting, because sparks from their weapons might ignite hydrogen which was pouring out of the gasbag valves as the ship rapidly rose!

It is a matter of the record that throughout the First World War, there was never a shortage of airship crews (all volunteers), even when the loss rate became horrific. Altogether over 1,500 German airshipmen were trained, half lost their lives through one cause or another.

Problems facing the wartime Zeppelin crews were formidable. Until 1915 no flying machines of any kind had made regular inter-country flights. Aerial navigation was unknown and no special maps existed. While the Zeppelins of DELAG had regularly flown for several hours over Germany, this was always in fair weather with good visibility, and familiar landmarks were plentiful such as the rivers, railways and townships. Flights above the North Sea had been conducted with the German High Seas Fleet, but again, never too far away from a known coastline.

Contrast this with an early wartime raid. Each Zeppelin was under the command of its captain, with a navigating officer on board. Leaving the continental coastline they flew out of sight of land and eventually crossed the English coast. But where? Airships, especially the early wartime ones, made an average of less than fifty mph, much less if flying against a stiff breeze. Their large side area made them susceptible to sideways drift in any wind other than one directly ahead or astern. All navigating officers were naval officers, experienced in marine methods of deduced reckoning. However, sea currents seldom exceeded five or six knots whereas winds could be variable, frequently gusting up to 25 knots. Thus the Zeppelin captain had to pinpoint a prominent feature over England before he was certain of his position.

Peacetime DELAG flights over Germany were conducted in daytime. Few night-time flights were undertaken. All the Zeppelin air-raids on Great Britain were carried out by night. By blacking out her towns and cities when a raid was forthcoming, wartime Britain further confounded her aerial invaders. Initially, much confusion reigned among the airship captains as to their true position at any given time, but by 1917, with the benefit of experience and the newly-formed radio location beacons, surviving crews had developed a more refined and accurate system. Zeppelins penetrated as far west as Liverpool and the Scottish Highlands but tended to get lost when away from the eastern coastline. Short nights in summer-time were not popular with the raiders. Unpredicted winds or failing engines could leave a Zeppelin crossing the coast for home in the morning light when it was a 'sitter' for the defences.

During moonlight nights, prominent landmarks stand out almost as well as during daylight. One of these was Flamborough Head, which became a popular entry point for Zeppelins raiding the north of England (as indeed it did for the Luftwaffe during the Second World War).

Consider the following account (extracted from the Public Records Office at Kew) by Oblt z S Richard Frey, Watch Officer on L.22, (commanded by KL Heinrich Hollender). It refers to his first operation over Britain on the night of 27/28 November 1916.

The hangars disappeared faster and faster from our view, and our ship slowly rose into the blue ether. It was an exceptionally fine autumn day, the sky was steel blue, without any clouds. The commander first ordered us to climb to 1,000 m, so that the ships should become somewhat heavier, as it was easier then to steer it, while at the same time it should not at once become light again through the consumption of petrol and oil. L.21 and L.34 had started with us from Nordholz (near Cuxhaven).

The short run from the land to the coast was taken advantage of to ascertain exactly the direction and strength of the wind, as this is of the utmost importance for navigation. Wind has an influence on the speed of the ship, and then if it strikes the ship at an angle to the direction of flight, there results a lateral deviation, commonly called drifting. This drifting must be taken into account in fixing the course, that is to say, I must make allowance accordingly, so as to reach the exact point I am making for.

We had soon flown over the East Frisian Islands and stood above the open North Sea. I now gave the order to prime the bombs. So long as the ship is over land, the fuses could not be screwed on, because it might happen that, for some reason or other, a bomb should fall. Thus, there could at least be no explosion. We are now making a westerly course, in order to make for England. Of course, it was necessary to keep a sharp look-out, as in the North Sea we must always reckon with the appearance of enemy fighting craft or submarines, which, if they should be recognised too late, might make things dangerous for the airship with their artillery. It was also necessary to watch for enemy aeroplanes. After a short time we caught sight of L.13, L.14 and L.16, which had started from Hage, in East Friesland, and later of L.24 from Tondern. Forming a bold front of seven airships, we then proceeded on our westward course. It was an impressive sight, which always remained with me during my later flights. No one at home had any idea of the forthcoming raid, and in England, no one had thought of it. However, the airships were going straight to their goal, and all the crews were filled, firm as a rock, with the will to bring death and ruin to proud England, through whose fault our poor people were suffering the bitterest privations.

The advance itself took a relatively long time, because, as I mentioned in the first instance, it was taking place against the wind. The greatest attention was given to navigation, as it was exceptionally important to ascertain the force and direction of the wind at various altitudes, so that we could absolutely reach our objective later when it was quite dark. We had not sighted any fighting craft of any kind, and the hours would not pass quickly enough for us. At last the sun disappeared below the horizon and twilight set in. As it became darker, the men grew more excited. Someone was constantly going to the steersman or coming to me, to enquire how long it would be before we reached the coast. Before darkness set in, I went once more over the ship, in order to make sure that everything was in order. This also took me to the rear car, where the engineer stood with three engine-room mates. The hellish noise which was going on in this car can only be realised by those who have stood in it. Three 240-hp engines, and in addition, the noise of the long shafts to the side propellers! L.22 was not yet provided with side engine-cars. It was impossible to hear one another, unless we shrieked in the other man's ear, or proceeded by signs. Hats off! to this excellent staff who performed their duty for twenty hours in this hell!!

When I returned, L.34, which was proceeding on our starboard, could still be dimly seen, but darkness soon concealed it from our eyes.

The airship was made quite invisible from the outside, only the compass, the altimetric barometer and the water gauge on the elevator were lit, but so that no light could be seen from the outside. The light in the chart-room, used for navigation purposes, switched off automatically when the door was opened. It was a wonderful winter night, absolutely star clear, without any clouds. The starry sky showed itself in the pure air of 2,000-m altitude with such magnificence as can never be seen from the earth. There was a very strong northern light towards the north sky, which resembled a bundle of rays from innumerable searchlights. The North Sea beneath us was a deep black.

At 9 p.m. we were, according to our reckoning, still about two hours from the coast, and the commander gave the order 'Clear the decks for the fight', and made the ship rise to 2,500 m, as we must now reckon with shooting from sea fighting craft. When this order was given, the fighting men in the steering-car took their posts at the elevators and side-rudders and the men in reserve did duty as look-outs. The engines were put to their maximum number of revolutions and switched on to full speed, which was shown by the small radium lines, so that the mistake of switching on weight lightening could not be made. In the gangway a non-com. took charge of the speaking-tube in the bomb-room, to make absolutely sure that every order would pass through the ship, even if the apparatus should fail. The bomb traps provided under the bombs were opened, so that bomb dropping could start immediately.

All eyes were fixed forward, as everyone wanted to be the first to sight the English coast. Then, suddenly, at 10 p.m., the fine sight of Flamborough Head came into sight so wonderfully clear that we should never have thought it to be possible. We were then still an hour away from the coast. With field glasses we could distinctly see the waves breaking against the cliffs on the coast. Both the commander and I began to be in doubt as to attacking in such clearness. It was obvious that our ship, with its light-coloured hull and the strong northern light prevailing, must show up against the dark sky. Moreover, we could at most reach an altitude of 3,000 metres. In view of the conditions of the English defences at this time, this was decidedly too low, especially as there were no clouds, by means of which we could temporarily disappear from view.

But their could be no question of turning back. The crews could never have understood it that the commander should now, in sight of the English coast, give the order to turn back, when we could at least experience our first raid on England. Well, let us go for the enemy then, it will soon be settled! We took the ship up to the raiding altitude which, in spite of the low temperature of 21 degrees Centigrade, only reached 2,900 metres, although we had thrown off

400 kilos of petrol to lighten it. We could see the land more and more distinctly, and by 11 p.m. we stood exactly over Flamborough Head.

The reception we received from the English was very different from what we should have imagined judging by the descriptions we had been given. Nothing moved. Underneath us was the country, exactly as on a map. It was so light that we could perfectly distinguish the country roads, watercourses, groups of trees and houses. The darkening of the houses was excellent, so not the least ray of light showed outside. Even while we were flying over the coast, no anti-aircraft guns or searchlights could be seen. I must candidly admit that this tranquillity made the commander and I feel uncomfortable. It made one feel that the English were saying 'Just come in, but you shan't go back'. Suddenly, a powerful searchlight came out, but only held the ship for quite a short time and then repeatedly played in the direction of our course through the sky. Then it went out again. This proceeding also had a peculiar effect on us. It must be undoubtably be a signal for the defending aeroplanes which were in the air, to show them the direction of our course. This meant that we had to redouble our vigilance.

The choice of the place to be raided was left by the F.d.L. entirely to the commander, because it was only on the spot that it was possible to fix the place to be raided, according to the weather conditions and the visibility to be found. We decided to raid the city of York, which we saw lying in front of us. The houses and factories were perfectly darkened, but owing to the light which prevailed, everything could be easily recognised, and the English helped us to find our objective, by erecting a ring of searchlights all around the town. All we had to do was to go inside this ring to find a sure target for our bombs. One of the Hage airships had already attacked the place before us, and left very large fires behind it. At this time L.13 stood over the town and was busy attacking. The airship was lit by a large number of searchlights and appeared vivid white against the dark sky; in addition, firing was very lively against it. It was an entrancing sight, this play of searchlights, the flash of the anti-aircraft guns and in between the explosion of the bombs and fires which broke out.

On our way to York, we passed over New Malton, where I perfectly distinguished a very large blast furnace establishment. The works buildings were completely darkened, but the glare of the fire in the blast furnace could not be concealed. I decided to drop my first bomb here and had the luck of making a very good hit, so that we were able to observe very big explosions in the blast furnaces. The bomb-dropping apparatus with the sighting telescope, was at the front of the steering-car, together with the side rudder. Dropping was operated electrically. By pressing on the dropping knob, the bolt of the bomb hook was released and the bomb fell through the air. This made it possible to drop the bombs one by one. If a good hit had been made, we could fire a volley of several bombs at once. Each bomb was shown on the apparatus by means of a small control lamp. For the 300 kg bombs I had a blue lamp, for 100 kg bombs they were green and for 50 kg bombs, red. I could thus ascertain at any time how many bombs of each kind were still on board.

When we made a good hit on the blast furnaces, peace was of course over for the English. They at once opened a strong fire from several batteries. One of these made itself very trying, but was soon silent again, after I had sent a 50 kg bomb down between its guns. At 12.25 a.m. we then proceeded with the raid on York. The effect of our bombs on the blast furnaces and factories was indeed excellent. We repeatedly noticed great explosions and saw many buildings fall in. The noise made by the anti-aircraft batteries, the bursting shells and the explosion of our own bombs, was simply indescribable. It seemed as if hell had been let loose. I had selected particularly good targets for my two 6 cwt bombs. The explosion of these bombs was so powerful that our airship, at an altitude of nearly 3,000 metres, received a violent shock. The engineer's mate at the foremost engine, ran into the steering-car saying that the car must have been hit from below.

By dropping bombs, our ship had been lightened by quite 2,000 kg, and we could now rise to 3,300 m, and this suited us very well, in view of the hefty firing of the anti-aircraft guns. Of course, we now turned as quickly as possible towards the coast. To the north we could again distinguish L.34, which apparently had taken part in the raid and was brilliantly lit by searchlights. The ship stood quite 4,000 metres high, as it carried a much greater load than our L.22. Heavy firing was directed against it. A short time after, we saw above the airship a red light appear, and immediately the searchlights went out and the artillery fire ceased. The red light must have been a signal, shown by an English aeroplane ready for the attack, so as not to be endangered by their own artillery and searchlights. We had already heard of this signal through our agent's reports, and I had therefore taken care that we too should have a few red signalling cartridges on board. This precaution should be very useful later on. A few minutes late, we suddenly saw on our stern, high up in the sky, a mighty blood-red flame appearing, and we soon had to recognise, unfortunately, that it was L.34 which had been set on fire by the English aeroplane. A gruesome picture of destruction that unfolded before our eyes. As hydrogen gas can only burn when mixed with air, the airship first burnt right along the whole top, because the air could reach there. Owing to loss of gas, it slowly became heavier and fell stern first downwards on account of its construction, so that it finally stood vertically in the air. As it sank to the ground, the heat caused by the burning of the gas had made the entire framework red-hot and this showed the form of the airship against the dark sky. We could thus follow the crash to the very end.

The enormous framework of the airship offered so much resistance to the air, that the crash did not proceed so quickly as one would have imagined. It certainly lasted several minutes, before the airship reached the ground. It crashed into the sea near the coast and we could clearly see how it broke in two pieces. The brave commander, capt-lieut, of the reserve Dietrich, and his observer, the first lieutenant, von Nathusius, RN Reserve, together with the whole of the brave crew, who had already gone through many raids on England safely, and whom we all knew well at Nordholz, thus met the death of heroes. But we had no time to mourn over our dear comrades, as we had to give the whole of our attention to our airship.

Our airship was then caught by three searchlights and held like iron. It was absolutely impossible to escape from the cone of light, as there were no clouds of any kind. The illumination was so brilliant that we could have read a newspaper in the ship, while at the same time wild firing commenced with guns of every calibre. As owing to this bright illumination, our 180-metre long ship formed quite an excellent target, the English very soon found the range. A hail of shrapnel, shells and incendiary bombs rained all around us. The thunder of the guns and the sharp report of the bursting shells was indescribable. It was a depressing feeling for us that we had no more bombs on board and could do nothing against the firing, except to make an attempt to come out of the range of fire as quickly as possible. The incendiary shells were the most unwelcome. Their calibre was about 15 cm, and they contained a red-hot fiery mass, so that their path could be seen perfectly. They repeatedly whizzed close above or under the ship, and we breathed again, each time they had cleared us. If one of then had hit us we should have shared the fate of our comrades of L.34.

To this must be added the well-found fear that the aeroplane which had brought down L.34 might now give its attention to us. The commander, therefore, ordered me to climb on the platform and repel aeroplanes from there with machine-guns. This was the only means of defence we had against attacking aircraft. The result was most doubtful, because, if an aeroplane stood once over the ship and the colossal target it presented, it would hardly be sent away by a machine-gun.

As it was bitterly cold, I had put on fur-lined boots and a heavy sheepskin. I had no idea then of what an exertion it would be, with these heavy things on, to climb through thin air the shaft 10 metres high, leading to the platform, which was built somewhere over the steering-car, on the top of the airship. The shaft led to the top between the gas-cells and had to be climbed by an aluminium ladder, the steps of which were quite half a metre apart. The heavy clothing weighed hundredweights on me, and I had to drag them up; moreover it was anything but pleasant, while the heavy firing was going on, to climb between the gas-cells. I was very glad when I at last saw the fine night sky above me.

The platform itself measured about two square metres, and is not provided with a railing of any kind. In the centre is the pivot for the machine-gun, to which one must hold on rather tightly. It was difficult to stand upright, as our speed was (we were now flying before the wind) quite 100 kilometres per hour, and one had to struggle against the rush of air. As I was looking downwards, I unintentionally made a step backwards, because an enormous searchlight was shining right in my face. The searchlights used by the English were of a much larger size than those used in our Fleet. The hail of shot was ever increasing. I could personally observe how a shrapnel hit the ship from above, while we received a second hit from below. Our chance of being shot down was practically certain, and then the commander thought of the red star signals I had taken on board. As a last resource, he wished to try the experiment. He had a star shell fired and, behold, the English allowed themselves to be deceived, think that a defensive aeroplane had shot the star, and the artillery fire ceased. When a second star was fired, the searchlights were also extinguished.

For the time being we were saved. The point was now to reach the coast as quickly as possible, before the English noticed the trick. We proceeded with our engines running at full capacity and passed over the coast at Hornsea at 1.25 a.m. Down below, they had vainly waited for us to be brought down, and they could see now they had been caught napping. The searchlights played about the sky, trying to find us. Fortunately a screen of mist formed between us and the coast, so the searchlights could no longer find us. The success of our raid was indisputable. When we were one and a half hours distant from the coast we could still recognise the enormous fires which we had kindled.

But we ourselves had suffered all round. When I came down again from the platform, the lighting plant failed on the airship. All our command apparatus, compass and altitude barometer, were without light, and our people necessarily had to resort to pocket lamps. The greatest inconvenience was caused by the loss of light in the wireless station (wireless room), where there was plenty for me to do for me now. In the first place, we had to wireless our report on the raid to the F.d.L, so the commander of the fleet and our leader should know where we had raided, and that we were on our way back.

Unfortunately, it was soon found that our ship was steadily increasing in weight. Owing to two hits by shrapnel, ten of our cells had been shot through, and gas was leaking from them steadily. Our sail-maker, chief-mate Wundrack, stepped in like a hero. He crept to the top of the ship, in order to stop the shot holes, as it was, of course, through the holes on top that most of the gas was escaping. It goes without saying that our position could not be much improved by this, as we had innumerable shrapnel holes in the cells. Later when we had returned to the hangar, it was found that there were about 150 holes.

Our ship was becoming more and more heavy and could hardly be steered. We therefore threw overboard two more petrol casks which we could spare, but we were very soon again in the same slanting position. Meanwhile I was endeavouring in the wireless station, with the wireless operators, to decipher the messages received, with the aid of a pocket lamp and the signal book. In this way we also received the report of the raids by the other ships, which had set out together with us, with the exception of L.21. This ship was also repeatedly called by the flagship of the fleet, but unfortunately without success. It was to be feared that it had also become the victim of the enemy's defence, and on returning to port, we heard to our regret that this was confirmed. 1/Lt R.N. Frankenberg and Lt RN Reserve Salzbrunn, had died like heroes with their brave crew.

Meanwhile, our position had become most critical. To make matters worse, one of our engines gave out, and this made the slanting position of our ship worse. If this was to go on, we could no longer hold up in the air and must sink into the North Sea, where we should meet the same fate as the L.19 did previously. We must do everything possible to obtain asistance from naval fighting craft, who could pick us up. I therefore signalled to the commander of the Fleet, telling him our position and asking to be taken up by naval fighting craft, as we were seriously damaged.

As the slanting position was becoming ever more threatening, we attempted to trim the ship and dragged along the gangway from aft to the most forward point everything weighty that could be spared. In the darkened gangway and owing to the heavy list of the ship, this was extraordinarily hard work. In order to understand it, I may mention that the gangway is a narrow board, only 20 cm wide, made of stretchers. Stepping aside meant at once crashing through the envelope into the depths. Therefore it was not quite a simple matter to move along the gangway in the dark and carrying loads.

We had given the engineers a definite time in which to repair the engine, otherwise, they were to dismantle it and throw it overboard. By good luck, they succeeded in repairing it, and then we had all the tools and all the machine spare parts thrown overboard, so that our position was once more improved to some extent. At last, the sun rose in a rosy light in the east, and this gave us fresh hopes and a new courage. After a little time, we could distinguish the East Frisian Islands, and then also sighted the great cruiser H.M. *Moltke*, with two smaller cruisers and a torpedo-boat flotilla sailing towards us, with the intention of picking us up.

Under the rays of the sun, our gas had become warmer and our carrying capacity had thereby increased. We therefore felt quite proud of ourselves and we wirelessed to the Fleet: 'Endeavouring to land at Hage on our own power.' Under no circumstance could we reach our own port, but we still had hopes of reaching Hage. At 8 a.m., we stood over the place. The question now was to lighten the ship as much as possible and consequently threw overboard all empty water sacks, fur coats, fur-lined boots and the like, and then our last two petrol casks, which crashed to the ground with a loud report. At 8.30 a.m. we could proceed with the landing and we let the ship fall on the ground with a weight of about 3000 kg. As we expected a heavy impact, we all stood kneeling lightly in the steering-car, while we sent all the crew that could be spared in the gangway, so that no one should be hurt unnecessarily. The landing squad behaved so excellently, however, that they caught the forward car quite smoothly. As regards the aft car, the ship landed on a post two metres high of the ground enclosure and rammed it completely into the earth. Anyway this damped our impact quite well, so that the operation went through somewhat gently. The shafts of the side propellers were bent and some rings had got broken in the frame, in addition to which some of the supports of the side propeller gearing were broken. None of the crew were hurt.

We had brought the ship safely into port and we rode into the hangar to the sound of the band.

Our crew had survived the baptism of fire and had brilliantly withstood the test. It was only due to the circumstance that every man had done his duty to the utmost and put all his strength in doing his task, that we safely came through this dangerous raid. We all, officers and men, had learnt a very great deal from this trip, and had gained full confidence in our ship and what we could do. The dangers through which we had gone together had bound us together more closely, and every man in the crew had now gained an unshakeable confidence in his leaders.

After three days, our ship was already repaired, and we could then again fly back to our home port Nordholz. There, of course, a thorough examination of our ship was again made, and all the gas-cells which had been shot through were carefully inspected, so that no hole should be overlooked. Quite a large number of shrapnel bullets were found in the cells. We also received special satisfaction from the fact that the F.d.L., in the order of the day, expressed to the officers and men of L.22, his full recognition of the fact that they had succeeded in bringing their severely damaged ship safely home.

L.13 – a similar Zeppelin to L.22 – in which Richard Frey served, and referred to in his account. Note machine-gun position on top of the hull, which was also mentioned. (*Ces Mowthorpe Collection*)

The above translation (reproduced exactly) is from an article written by Richard Frey and published in *Deutsche Zeitung* in May 1927. Despite the dramatic rhetoric and somewhat dated prose it is the best-known account of a Zeppelin in action over Britain. For the record there were no blast furnaces at New Malton. What Richard Frey had seen was the municipal gasworks. Looking downwards at a slow speed they would see the fires which produced the local community gas. Other Zeppelin crews made similar mistakes. Despite the account of the bombing of York, it is a matter of the record that the group of Zeppelins which attacked York (and the Midlands) all crossed the coast between Spurn and Filey i.e., near Flamborough Head. Most of the bombing was aimless, although one attack on the Potteries by L.21 caused a little damage but no casualties (she paid for her audacity by crossing the coast near Yarmouth at 0605 hrs in the light of dawn, being shot down by Flt Sub Lt Pulling and Flt Lt Cadbury). Four fatalities and thirty-two injured, were, however, reported in Hartlepool.

It was such highly dramatic reports made by returning Zeppelin captains, which encouraged the Germans to continue their raids in the face of horrific losses. While this book is not about war, great credit must be given to all the German airship crews who pioneered long-distance flight in airships, performing feats of navigation and endurance impossible by any other means.

Both Richard Frey and his commander, Heinrich Hollender survived the war. The naval Zeppelin L.22 was shot down over the North Sea by Flt Lt Galpin and Flt Sub Lt Leckie in a flying-boat from Great Yarmouth on 14 May 1917.

Count Zeppelin's giant airships dominated the German lighter-than-air scene throughout the First World War. However, the Zeppelin company were not the only builders of giant airships for Germany.

Professor Johannes Shütte was a trained naval architect, a graduate of the University of Danzig. Initially a great friend and adviser of the count, they fell out because Count Zeppelin was a stubborn character and refused to acknowledge Professor Shutte's suggestions which were based upon scientific calculation. Consequently, Shütte teamed up with the Karl Lanz company and began building rigid airships to his own design. Known as the Shütte-Lanz airships, a total of twenty were built and flown prior to the Armistice.

Unlike the Zeppelins, the Shütte-Lanz ships were of wooden construction, that is, the radial frames and lengthwise longitudinals were formed from high quality spruce, or similar. Actually quite a lot of metal was incorporated. For example, to improve rigidity, the completed framework was tightly bound with miles of wire, plus other various metal fittings. The result was a very efficient airship. Combined with a flush-fitting control-car and improved fins and rudders, these wooden ships out-performed their Zeppelin counterparts in the air.

Sadly, being of wooden construction they did not stand up to the harsh realities of service conditions, especially when operated in the cold moist North Sea air. The special Kaline glue was affected by salt air and consequently fractured parts became commonplace. No ships was lost through this weakness but compared with the aluminium/duralimin framed Zeppelins they were, service-wise, unsuitable. Relegated to the Eastern Front and training, these wooden monsters gave only fair operational service.

SL.X1 was the first German airship shot down over Britain on 3 September 1916 by Captain Leefe-Robinson. The story of Herr Müller's stealing the plans of the (then) latest Shütte-Lanz airship is told on p. 00. Hence the British R.31 and R.32 were basically Shütte-Lanz designs.

A little-realised fact is that although German airships flew hundreds of operations bombing Britain, they flew four times as many operations over the North Sea in conjunction with the German Navy: mainly reconnaissance flying. Bear in mind that it is almost as useful for an Admiral to know where the enemy is not – as to know where he is.

On one occasion a Zeppelin put men onto an enemy ship and forced the crew to sail to a German port. Expecting to be praised for his actions, the Zeppelin commander was severely reprimanded for 'hazarding his airship'! Chief of Naval Airship Service, Peter Strasser, icily remarked that he did not expect his commanders to risk a valuable airship and trained crew, for the sake of capturing an insignificant trading vessel!

Despite all their losses, the German nation had an expertise in operating large rigid ships which was to stand them in good stead after the war. They operated two civil airships in 1919–20 but as the Allies then placed an embargo upon all flying, it was not until the LZ-126 (ZR-3 was her American designation – and named *Los Angeles*) was built, sold and flown to America in 1925, that their amazing between-the-wars operations started.

No book about airshipmen would be complete without mentioning three very remarkable men who escaped from blazing Zeppelins, which had fallen thousands of feet after being attacked by British warplanes.

At 0150 hrs on the morning of 7 June 1915 the German Army Zeppelin LZ-37 was returning from a raid on Dover, under the command of Oblt Otto von der Haegen. Obersteuermann Alfred Muhler was the steering coxswain in the forward gondola. Lt Warneford of the Royal Naval Air Service was meanwhile flying a Morane monoplane on an anti-Zeppelin patrol at 8,000 ft near LZ-37's base, the Brussels-Etterbeek shed. Warneford's first attack was beaten off by LZ-37's top gunners but biding his time, Warneford climbed steadily, keeping the enemy in sight. At 0215 hrs the Zeppelin was approaching Ghent and proceeded to lose height in preparation for landing. Lt Warneford saw his opportunity and dived along the top of the airship, releasing his four 20-lb anti-Zeppelin bombs. LZ-37 erupted in flames, gas-cells exploding, her shattered framework falling on top of a convent in Ghent. Meanwhile Obersteuermann Muhler, aware of his terrible fate, remained conscious in the control gondola throughout. Seeing his captain and fellow crew either dead or unconscious, Muhler was on the verge of passing out when he felt a terrible impact as the doomed Zeppelin hit the convent. Muhler then found himself deposited upon a bed – under the gaze of a terrified nun. Severely burnt and with other minor injuries, Alfred Muhler lived on, surviving both world wars.

Two more extraordinary survivals came on the 17 June 1917 when the Naval Super-Zeppelin L.48, under the command of Korvettenkapitan Viktor Schutze attacked Harwich. Her executive officer was Otto Miech. L.48 was attacked by several aeroplanes and finally Lt Watkins, RFC set the airship on fire with his incendiary bullets. Otto Miech was in the control gondola and looking aft, saw the 600-ft airship ablaze. He records that Captain Schutze stood firm and motionless, staring at the flames then turned to him (Miech) and calmly said 'It's all over.' Suddenly the ship lurched violently and started falling stern first. This threw the control-car crew into one corner with Miech at the bottom of the heap. In the horrendous heat from the flames, Miech lost consciousness. The shock of the stricken vessel hitting the ground brought Miech temporarily round. He recalls crawling away from the wreckage before again passing out. Another crewman, Heinrich Ellerkamm, was found wandering around the wreckage apparently uninjured except for minor burns. Both Miech and Ellerkamm were hospitalised, interrogated and interned before finally being repatriated after the Armistice. Sadly, a third member of L.48, Machinist's Mate Wilhelm Uecker was dragged alive from the starboard engine car but suffered severe internal injuries from which he died some weeks later.

Machinist's mate Heinrich Ellerkamm, still alive in the 1960s, related his experience in a German magazine:

> The English intercepted a message to us (L.48) requesting that we descend to 3400 m where we would find a favourable wind. My chief, who was making his rounds advised us (in the engine-car) of this message, five minutes before the attack.
>
> We were on our way home and I was checking the fuel in the tank above our motor car. Standing on the open ladder between the car and the hull I heard machine-gun fire. Climbing into the hull, I was stood on the walkway looking aft when phosphorous bullets came tearing through the gas-cells. I was horrified. This was the finish of us.
>
> There was an explosion, a large 'woof,' like when you light a large gas stove. I watched in horror as one gas-cell after another exploded into flame. Panic-stricken I climbed higher and higher into the airship's framework to avoid the flames. My fur coat was burning and I

tried to beat the flames with one hand. The weight of the large two-engined rear gondola was dragging down by the stern and the ship fell vertically, flame roaring above my head and the wind whistling through the framework. The draught was blowing the flames away from me and I was thinking of letting go and falling rather than roasting to death. Still wavering, I became aware of something below and outside of the falling ship. There was a terrible smashing of metal and I found myself flung to the ground. Trapped in a cage of red-hot girders, with oil from bursting tanks all around, I forced my way through the girders and fell breathless onto cool wet grass. My hands were terribly burnt with flesh hanging down but I felt no pain until in hospital the next day.

After the end of the war, stories were circulated that Zeppelin crews carried poisoned tablets and pistols to shoot themselves, should they find themselves in the position that I did that night. This is not true. We Zeppelin crewmen knew the risks and were prepared to die for our country like the patriots we were.

By October and November 1918, the once proud German Navy was in the throes of a rebellion. Subversive literature and rebel leadership established Soldiers' and Sailors' Councils, who took control away from naval officers in the name of The Sailors' Soviet. Many sailors stood behind their officers but with defeat established, all control was lost. All the Zeppelin bases were guarded by the Sailors' Soviet during December 1918 but the airshipmen themselves stood loyal to their seniors.

Regular professional officers and crewmen still remaining on the airship bases, deflated their Zeppelins, leaving them suspended by ropes from the roof trusses and resting upon blocks beneath. These airshipmen never once turned away from their established discipline, obedient and quietly keeping some order in the midst of virtual chaos.

Many schemes were discussed and cast aside but when the German High Sea Fleet carried out its scuttling at Scapa Flow, right under the nose of their victors, on 21 June 1919, the decision to act swiftly and surely was taken. Officers and men at Nordholz, Wittmundhaven and Alhorn bonded together, swearing never to reveal names of any of the conspirators. Two nights later on 23 June at midnight, they quietly entered the huge sheds and taking away the blocks beneath the giant airships, cut the ropes securing them to the roof, the huge monsters crashing twelve foot to the ground, causing irreparable damage to their hulls.

A German Zeppelin lies wrecked in her Nordholz shed. She had been dropped from her roof suspensions after deflation – about 7 m – by her crew (with another seven Zeppelins) at midnight on 23 June 1919, to prevent her falling into 'the enemy's hands'. For the same reason the German High Seas Fleet had scuttled itself at Scapa Flow a few days earlier. (*Ces Mowthorpe Collection*)

All the Nordholz Zeppelins were destroyed, L.14, L.41, L.42, L.63 and L.65. Wittmundhaven destroyed her two ships L.52 and L.56 but at Alhorn, where the latest design of Zeppelin, L.71, together with L.64 were housed, the plan was revealed to the Sailors' Soviet, who picketed the sheds, thus preventing airshipmen entering to scuttle these two ships.

German airshipmen never betrayed their country, neither did they betray the 'saboteurs' who scuttled the proud fleet of Zeppelins. Today, in the 1990s, all will be dead and never will their names be known. Many years later, when the *Graf Zeppelin* was proving to the world the benefit (in the 1930s) of airship travel, word was passed around that the scuttling of the wartime Zeppelins was more a protest against the hated communist regime, than against the victorious Allies.

From 24 August 1919 until 5 December 1919 the reconstituted DELAG company operated a small Zeppelin, built from their existing stocks of Duralumin and engines, on a schedule service to Berlin Staaken. Similar in size to the pre-war *Sachsen* she was named *Bodensee*. Powered by four 245-hp wartime Maybachs, a speed of 82 mph was obtained. Her combined control-car and passenger cabin had seating for 20 passengers (six extra wicker seats could be placed in the aisle under favourable conditions). With full wireless communication and a small kitchen for the chef, flights were safe and pleasurable, cutting

These two small passenger-carrying Zeppelins *Bodensee* (above) and *Nordstern* (below) were built in 1919 from parts of unassembled wartime Zeppelins. *Bodensee* particularly carried out many profitable flights and was joined briefly in 1919 by her sister-ship. Then the victorious Allies put a stop to this enterprise, both ships being given to Allied powers as war retributions. *Nordstern* can be identified by her slightly larger passenger-car. (*Ces Mowthorpe Collection*)

the time between Friedrichshafen and Berlin to six hours, as against sixteen by train. Operating alternate days in each direction, time was often found to carry out an evening sightseeing trip for the Berliners. Producing profits, without subsidies, DELAG had a sister-ship built for the 1920 season named *Nordstern* but the Inter-Allied Commission of Control claimed them as compensation, thus the 1920 season never got underway. *Nordstern* was given to France and *Bodensee* to Italy in 1921. Neither of these small Zeppelins were flown much by their 'captors', both being eventually broken up.

CHAPTER SEVEN

Zeppelins Between the Wars

Under the impetus of the First World War, all forms of flying made tremendous strides. A Vickers 'Vimy', piloted by Alcock and Brown successfully crossed the Atlantic in 1919. The RAF operated a very efficient Forces mail service throughout Northern Europe. These operations, good as they were, fell far short of profitable long-range people carriers. Aeroplanes were improving but the large rigid airship appeared to be the answer. Zeppelins made regular eight- and ten-hour flights during wartime, returning safely to their bases, unless prevented by the enemy.

Two well-recorded and remarkable Zeppelin flights proved this. On 26 July 1917, Oblt z.S. Ernst Lehmann (later to command the LZ-129 *Hindenburg*) took the Army Zeppelin LZ-120 from her shed at Seerappen and flew for 101 hours, landing safely back at Seerappen in the early hours of 31 July. She avoided bad weather, free-ballooned while men unlaced the outer cover and repaired a broken propeller bracket, on two separate occasions, before resuming flight across the western Baltic. When she finally landed there was still over ten hours' fuel left. The crew stood six-hour watches and slept in hammocks slung alongside the internal walkway. Lehmann was a very experienced captain who after the war became Dr Eckener's chief pilot on the commercial Zeppelins.

On 21 November 1917, the specially modified naval Zeppelin L.59 departed from her shed at Yambol in Bulgaria in an attempt to take urgently needed supplies of ammunition and medical equipment to General von Lettow-Vorbeck, who was fighting superior British forces in German East Africa. Carrying 47,000 lb of petrol, 16 tons of cargo and a crew of 22, this giant airship flew over the Gulf of Kos, Crete, Mersa Matruh in North Africa, the Sahara Desert, the Nile and down to Khartoum. Here a wireless message was received, apparently from Berlin, stating that von Lettow-Vorbeck had surrendered. This was a British intelligence trick – von Lettow-Vorbeck in fact, never surrendered until after the Armistice. L.59's Commander, Kapitanleutnant Bockholt made the difficult decision to turn about and fly back to Yambol. The return flight was accomplished safely and in the afternoon of 25 November, L.59 was back in her shed.

Today's traveller will perhaps see nothing outstanding about this flight but remember that in 1917 it was a tremendous feat – carried out as a more or less routine operation, by an airship and crew. Admittedly the L.59 had been modified to the extent of adding two 15-m cells to a standard 'v' class Zeppelin (incidentally making her the largest in the world at that time) plus increased fuel capacity. In all other respects she was a normal six-engined Zeppelin. While crossing Africa L.59 was subject to several violent thunderstorms. She travelled from the relatively cool Bulgarian climate right into equatorial Africa and back again – no mean feat in an airship which depends upon gas-cells to keep it airborne. Aloft for 95 hours, she had covered 4,250 miles. It was calculated that she still had fuel for a further 64-hours' flight, after being put into her shed at Yambol.

The Armistice and its consequences to the Zeppelin company halted all development in Germany. However, Great Britian had made considerable progress in the field of large rigids. R.33 and R.34, copies of Zeppelins brought down over England during the war and far behind the latest Zeppelins, were nevertheless successful. R.34 carried out a 56-hour flight over the Baltic and back in early 1919 and in July of that year departed RAF East Fortune in Scotland for Roosevelt Field, Long Island, New York with 30 persons plus one stowaway – a journey which took 108 hours. Mission accomplished, R.34 was moored outside (no shed was available in America) for three days and then departed Roosevelt Field, landing at RAF Pulham 75 hours later. Thus was the first double-crossing of the Atlantic Ocean achieved, carrying 30 persons with ease. Despite the many difficulties on the Atlantic flights, all overcome, it established that rigid airships were, at that period, the only effective means of intercontinental flights.

America showed great interest in the giant rigid airship. Her east and west coastlines bordered two vast oceans and the need for long-range aerial reconnaissance was paramount. A British rigid, R.38 was

ZR-1 *Shenandoah* riding to the Lakehurst high mast. Until her sad demise this airship performed excellently and laid the foundation for the great rigid programme which followed. (*Wg Cdr Dunn via Ces Mowthorpe Collection*)

bought from the Royal Airship Works at Cardington but met a tragic demise in 1921, while undergoing trials. Meanwhile a design and construction programme for an American-built ship had got under way. Using an ex-Zeppelin flight test captain and a British constructional engineer (who, incidentally worked together in the greatest harmony), the American designer produced an efficient craft, inflated with helium (of which at that time, America had a monopoly). Designated ZR-1 and christened *Shenandoah*, this ship was basically a copy of the latest wartime German Zeppelins plus a few modifications. She made her maiden flight in September 1923.

Since 1919, the Zeppelin Company had been trying to sell one of their ships to America. Bypassing the strict Allied military commission rules which prevented them building airships for themselves, it would mean survival of the Zeppelin company. The loss of the British-built ZR-2, enabled America to force British support for the purchase of a German Zeppelin and contracts were signed in June 1922. French insistence on various details meant that this would be a 'civil ship' (no armaments) and only the minimum safe size to make an Atlantic crossing.

Now the expertise of the German airshipmen could be revealed. Their wartime experience enabled them to design and build one of the two greatest Zeppelins in the world; the LZ-126, (ZR-3 in the American Navy and christened *Los Angeles*), 658 ft long, powered by five Maybach 400-hp motors which gave her a cruising speed of 70 mph. The 75 ft long gondola had the control-room in the front, behind were five staterooms, seating thirty passengers or twenty overnight passengers if the settees were converted into sleeping berths. A suitable kitchen and washrooms were provided. Though destined for military use, the *Los Angeles* would have made an excellent airliner. Initially inflated with hydrogen, when accepted by the American Navy she was re-inflated with helium.

This magnificent airship first flew in August 1924 and went on to fly a further four trial flights, prior to crossing the Atlantic. Naturally every opportunity was taken on these trials to display the Zeppelin to the maximum, routing over centres of population – thus restoring some Germanic pride after their wartime defeat.

Dr Eckener, that most experienced Zeppelin captain, was in command and preparations were made for the Atlantic crossing. Thirty-three tons of fuel were to be carried, a crew of twenty-seven and four passengers – American military officers. Today, as hundreds of jetliners cross the ocean, carrying thousands of passengers, it is

ZR-3 *Los Angeles* in flight. Built as the Zeppelin LZ-126, she was flown across the Atlantic to be used by the American Navy. This ship and her similar sister-ship, the German Zeppelin LZ-127 *Graf Zeppelin*, were the two most successful rigid airships ever flown and a credit to the Zeppelin designers. (*Ces Mowthorpe Collection*)

difficult to appreciate what a great undertaking this flight was in 1924. It should be remembered that this was not just an Atlantic crossing – it was from Friedrichshafen to Lakehurst, New York. Friedrichshafen is on Lake Constance near the Swiss border, in the centre of Europe. Also, because of prevailing weather patterns, the westward crossing was by far the most difficult.

Lifting off on 12 October, Dr Eckener flew a southern route, skirting a low pressure area situated in the North Atlantic (twenty years later, during the Seond World War this became known as 'pressure-pattern' flying), crossing France and exiting the mainland at the mouth of the Gironde. The Azores was sighted next day and the ship was fighting a 35 mph wind. It was realised that to press on directly into this wind meant that LZ-126 would not have enough fuel to reach America. Two USN cruisers, stationed in mid-Atlantic reported a low-pressure system south of Newfoundland. Dr Eckener took the bold decision to steer a northerly course which would later get into a favourable wind around this low pressure. Next day, Eckener found the headwind decreasing and was soon into a favourable tailwind. This gave a groundspeed of 78 mph on half power and in the early morning of 15 October, lights of a large town were seen on the horizon, proving to be Boston. At 0930 hrs LZ-126 made a safe descent onto Lakehurst after a 5,000-mile flight, taking 81 hours at an average speed of 61 mph, Dr Eckener and his crew were received with great enthusiasm by the American people. The LZ-126 was repainted in American colours and re-inflated with helium – going on to fly for another eight years, making 328 flights totalling 4,093 flying hours: a truly remarkable feat for that period. Decommissioned at the end of 1932, then scrapped, she trained a generation of American airshipmen without a single loss of life.

The transatlantic flight received world acclaim. Dr Eckener, now chairman of the Zeppelin company was upheld as the key to intercontinental air travel. The airship, slow by today's standards, with its 70 mph cruise was still more than twice as fast as surface shipping – cutting the Atlantic crossing by 50 per cent. October 1925 saw the signing of the Treaty of Locarno which among other matters, rescinded the ban on German airships. Now was the time to cash in. Dr Eckener, ably assisted by other wartime Zeppelin captains, Lehmann, von Schiller, Flemming, Pruss and Wittemann – all of whom had partaken in the Atlantic flight – raised over 2,500,000 marks by giving lectures, exhibitions etc. This enabled a start to be made on a new intercontinental commercial Zeppelin. The German government added a further 1,000,000 marks, enabling the craft to be completed. She was the LZ-127, christened *Graf Zeppelin*.

Basically the same design as the LZ-126 *Los Angeles*, LZ-127 *Graf Zeppelin* incorporated an extra section amidships, giving her a total gas volume of almost 4,000,000 cu ft. There was another significant difference. The ingenious airshipmen at Friedrichshafen had solved one of the great problems associated with lighter-than-air powered flight. Fuel, usually petrol, was consumed in huge quantities – 32 tons being required to fly the LZ-127 for 100 hours. This meant that as the ship became lighter she had to be constantly retrimmed by valving hydrogen. To compensate, large amounts of ballast were carried in case circumstances necessitated a sudden need for maximum lifting power. The Maybach engineers developed their engines to run (after being started with petrol) on 'Blau gas'. This weighed the same as air. *Graf Zeppelin* incorporated twelve 'Blau gas-cells', totalling approximately 900,000 cu ft below her hydrogen-filled cells. While this reduced the total lift, the advantages it conferred greatly improved the overall performance. Above the 'Blau gas-cells', slightly below the centre-line was another 'first', a walkway, which enabled riggers to examine all the gas-cells and the hydrogen cells valves relatively easily.

Graf Zeppelin carried crew and passengers in a large gondola, 99 ft long and 20 ft wide. Right forward was the control-car, flanked to port by a radio room, to starboard, a comprehensive galley. Behind these was the lounge, 16 ft × 16 ft, complete with four tables and sixteen chairs. Further aft, were five pairs of sleeping cabins, each with two bunks while at the extreme rear were washrooms and toilets. The crew were accommodated inside the hull proper, slinging hammocks over the lower gangway, etc. LZ-127 was designed to give a standard of travel almost equivalent to that of a first-class ocean liner.

Graf Zeppelin's first flight was on 18 September 1928, followed by four more, all relatively short. The first three used petrol only for the engines but on the fourth Blau Gas was carried and used successfully. On 2 October L-127 carried out a 34-hour trial. Crossing Holland she flew over the North Sea to Lowestoft, the first Zeppelin to fly to England since the war, returning to her shed via Kiel, Hamburg and Berlin. This flight caused two political outbursts, both serious. First, the French Government censured Dr Eckener for crossing the Rhineland. Second, the German Government accused him of over-flying Doorn in Holland, where the ex-Kaiser was in exile. This was a foretaste of the political wrangling which would bedevil Dr Eckener, and the Zeppelin company throughout its life.

Now commenced nine years of pioneering passenger-flying, not only across the Atlantic with fare-paying passengers, but a complete circumnavigation of the globe in August 1929. April 1931 saw the ship making a cruise over Egypt and the near East, in July a complete scientific and survey flight of the Arctic. August, September and October of that year saw three inaugural and scheduled flights to South America. Never before in history had an aircraft proved so versatile and reliable. Dr Eckener and his crew were fêted and respected throughout the world. The Germans, capitalising upon their wartime experience had developed superb navigation standards, using the latest in radio equipment to pioneer new standards of aviation safety. Dr Eckener himself, was a keen small-boat sailor as a boy. This inbred capacity to 'read the weather' coupled with advanced meteorological forecasts available by radio, enabled him to steer his airship around dangerous storms.

Financing the running of the *Graf Zeppelin* was initially a formidable task but nothing succeeds like success and as her reputation grew, so did the demand for her services. The transatlantic journeys became fully booked, thus gradually the enterprise became profitable. Further useful revenue was the carriage of mail – an onboard franking machine ensured that collectors worldwide paid an additional premium. During 1934 and 1935 twelve scheduled crossings of the South Atlantic took place each year, terminating at

LZ-127 *Graf Zeppelin* coming in to land at Friedrichshafen, *c.* 1936. The two giant airship sheds were called 'Luftschiff-halles', and in the new right-hand shed the nearly completed LZ-129 *Hindenburg* can be seen. (*Ces Mowthorpe Collection*)

Santa Cruz, Rio, in Brazil, where the government had established an airship base with shed and mast. This was in addition to the original simple mast at Recife. These crossings took place at fortnightly intervals during the summer months.

An interesting sidelight is this extract from *Flight* dated 21 March 1929: 'The fares for the coming flight of the *Graf Zeppelin*, from Germany to New York, due to start in May have been fixed at £400 for the single journey and £800 for the return journey.' It was a tremendous lot of money in 1929, but this was for the premium flight. Later, standard fares were fixed at £40 single and £80 return.

The *Graf Zeppelin* established a standard of long-range reliability, comfort and safety unsurpassed by any other aircraft, for many years to come. Much was made of the issue that no passenger had ever been lost in a Zeppelin airship. Aeroplanes crashed regularly, many with passengers, but not the Zeppelins. Their safety procedures were honed to a fine art, based upon their wartime military operations. All crews and passengers wore special rubber shoes (provided by the company), all matches, lighters, cigarettes, pipes and other inflammable material were impounded by the captain as passengers entered and returned when they landed. Even the machinists and crew had special tools which could not cause a spark if dropped. Gas purity in each cell was carefully monitored. Hence the disciplined procedures undertaken by the highly trained crews.

Political pressure was forever present. The German government had provided a million marks towards the cost and duly expected to profit from its investment, not financially, but nationally. Germany needed a success story after her defeat, which was followed by raging inflation. The Zeppelin company provided that success. Internationally courted for their expertise in construction and operation, especially in the Americas, they represented all that was good and great in Germany. Sadly, with the rise to power of Adolf Hitler and his fascist regime, this was to end. Despite protests from Dr Eckener, large swastikas were painted upon the huge tail surfaces, providing almost world-wide propaganda for the Nazi party. Dr Eckener's world-wide denouncement of the Nazis was well known. That he was not 'executed' in some manner can only be put down to his universal popularity. In 1935 Dr Eckener complained that his Zeppelin was being misused. Government funding had enabled the building of another airship, and LZ-129 *Hindenburg* was launched, larger than the *Graf Zeppelin*. It too was festooned with the swastika. On Hitler's orders the two giant airships flew over Nazi celebrations, sometimes dropping leaflets and addressing crowds through loudspeakers. Eckener's international protests resulted in him being removed from his position as head of the Zeppelin company. In

LZ-129 *Hindenburg* flying over the Brandenburg Gate in Berlin during a Nazi propaganda flight, with swastikas on the tail surfaces. It was 1937, the year that Germany hosted the Olympic Games, and the circles of the Olympic Games symbol were painted above the forward engine-car. (*Ces Mowthorpe Collection*)

March 1936 his position was taken by Ernest Lehmann. Never again was Dr Eckener allowed to voice an opinion, or take part, in that to which he had contributed so much.

Now is perhaps a good time to revue Dr Eckener's career. No one will dispute that he was the greatest rigid airship captain – his aviation career began when as a 30-year-old married man he was asked to write an article for the *Frankfurter Zeitung* about the first Zeppelin which was to make its second flight in October 1900. He was again requested to report to the same newspaper in November 1905 and January 1906 when the much modified Zeppelin again took the air over Lake Constance. His newspaper article attracted the attention of Count Zeppelin himself, who invited Dr Eckener to visit him. This meeting changed Eckener's life. As the Zeppelins, after many setbacks, became viable propositions, the formation of the commercial firm DELAG took place. Eckener had been manager of the Zeppelin Airship Co Ltd since September 1908 and was by now conversant with the piloting of these early airships, although not a qualified pilot. DELAG, the commercial Zeppelin company commenced operations with the L.7, a specially-built passenger airship. As related earlier, an ex-Army airship pilot and two ex-service helmsmen were employed, instructed by Count Zeppelin himself. After the demise of this airship, fortunately with no serious injuries, Dr Eckener qualified as a pilot and undertook, with the Count, the training of all future crews. Dr Eckener was responsible for the demise of the *Ersatz Deutschland* in May 1911, and this caused the doktor to re-evaluate Zeppelin operations. Without a doubt it was his meticulous attention to all details concerning the procedures of Zeppelin airships, which contributed to their huge successs. He personally trained most of the original airship captains, both civil and military. At the outbreak of war he was placed in charge of all military airship training.

The wealth of experience gained in wartime was brought together by Eckener and senior surviving wartime colleagues. The execution of the transatlantic flight of the *Los Angeles* and the later exploits of the *Graf Zeppelin* made his name a household word throughout the western world. As a young man he had sailed extensively in the Baltic and it was this in-built knowledge of metrology which stood him in good stead later. He, more than any other single man, developed the art of rigid airship flying. Never taking risks, a firm believer in strict discipline among his crews and using every single piece of modern equipment which the ingenious German engineers could devise, elevated him to a higher position by far, than the most senior captain of a 1990 wide-jet airliner.

Airshipmen, generally, never worried unduly about flying beneath thousands of cubic feet of hydrogen. On many occasions Dr Eckener was asked if he considered this dangerous. His stock reply was: 'Every motorist drives his car with gallons of inflammable petrol swilling around in his petrol tank. Does the motorist consider this danger? In my opinion it is more dangerous by far, than flying in a Zeppelin airship kept aloft by hydrogen gas.'

Lufthansa, the German national airline had started mail flights across the south Atlantic in the early 1930s, using Dornier flying-boats catapulted from special catapult ships, situated in mid-ocean. While these catapult ships were temporarily withdrawn for overhaul, the *Graf Zeppelin* overflew Bathurst (in 1997, Banjul) in Gambia, West Africa, during her (by now) normal, South American transatlantic service and dropped mail by parachute onto the Bathurst airfield. Circling the airfield again and hovering head to wind, the airship then lowered a line onto which were hooked several bags of mail. These were hoisted aboard and after a final circuit of the town the airship flew on. Dates were 16, 24 and 30 November 1935; 22 October, 13, 22 and 27 November 1936. *Graf Zeppelin* flew all the 1935 flights and the 22 November visit of 1936. *Hindenburg* flew the rest.

Following the successes of *Graf Zeppelin* and her predecessor *Los Angeles*, the German government and Württemberg State provided funds to erect a huge constructional shed at Friedrichshafen, 837 ft long, 164 ft wide and 164 ft high. This enabled Dr Eckener to build two giant airships, the LZ-129 and LZ-130 both of which were to be utilised on the transatlantic routes. Larger than any airship built, they had a length of 804 ft and diameter of 135 ft – longer than an ocean liner – with a gas capacity of 7,062,000 cu ft. Power was supplied by four Daimler-Benz 16-cylinder diesel engines of 1,300 hp. *Hindenburg* reverted to diesel engines instead of the Blau Gas used on the Graf because a system of recovering rainwater from the envelope (incidentally, this was a British invention) avoided the carrying of unnecessary water ballast. LZ-129 went into service, LZ-130 being completed after the LZ-129 *Hindenburg* disaster in May 1937 and was only used for research into British radio location by the German military authorities.

These magnificent airships were the culmination of thirty years' continuous Zeppelin construction and the experience gained in the

Passengers relaxing in the saloon of the LZ-129 *Hindenburg* during a transatlantic flight. Note the specially built aluminium grand piano in the corner. (*Ces Mowthorpe Collection*)

building of 118 airships. Their passenger compartments were all built into the lower hull on two decks. The upper had a dining-room, saloon and separate lounge – complete with special light alloy Steinway piano, plus twenty-five two-berth cabins, each with wash-basin. Below were situated wash-rooms, galley and a gas-tight smoking-room where the electric cigar/cigarette lighter was chained to a table and the entry doors had a pressurised passageway in between. This small passageway was constantly kept at several pounds per square inch pressure, greater than the rest of the interior. Hence no gas of any sort could enter the smoking-room.

It had been intended to inflate these two monsters with helium gas imported from America. Sadly, at the last moment, because of the Fascist regime in Germany, America backed out. *Hindenburg* was inflated with hydrogen which made her very 'light' (hydrogen having greater lifting power than the non-inflammable helium, for which she was designed). During the winter of 1936/7, *Hindenburg* was modified by the addition of nine more cabins, increasing her passenger capacity to seventy. Unfortunately this airship, like the ocean liner Titanic, was doomed.

After a satisfactory first flight of the 1937 season to Rio, this 'Southern route' to Rio was carried on by the older *Graf Zeppelin*. Returning to the new Zeppelin base at Frankfurt LZ-129 was prepared for the first of eighteen scheduled flights to Lakehurst, America. On this trip she carried only thirty-six passengers but had a 'double crew' of sixty-one, made up of an 'extra' training crew for the

LZ-130, also called *Graf Zeppelin* (not *Graf Zeppelin 2* as it is often erroneously stated), is shown here on one of her rare flights. Had the *Hindenburg* not crashed in 1937, the LZ-127 (original) *Graf Zeppelin* would have been taken out of service when LZ-130 took over. Although a sister-ship to *Hindenburg*, LZ-130 had a few differences. Her motors had tractor propellers – one of the very few airships to use these, and this was the first Zeppelin with tractor props. (*Ces Mowthorpe Collection*)

new LZ-130. Arriving safely at Lakehurst on the evening of 6 May 1937 the *Hindenburg* stood off for two hours avoiding a thunderstorm. When she eventually came in to land she burst into flames, crashing onto the field as a tangle of twisted girders. I believe she succumbed to that old enemy of hydrogen-filled airships, static electricity – but sabotage was also suspected. This accident was captured, as it happened, on movie film and distributed world wide. Brought face to face with a blazing airship collapsing onto the ground, the world was horrified and it sounded the death-knell for Zeppelins. Dr Eckener carried out his final task for the Zeppelin Co when he persuaded von Schiller not to make any more flights in the *Graf Zeppelin* until non-inflammable helium was available. The Second World War intervened before negotiations over the helium supply was complete and hence, for all practical purposes the era of the rigid airship came to an end.

One important point always overlooked in the *Hindenburg* disaster is that out of the ninety-seven souls on board, sixty-two survived, albeit some were terribly injured. Nevertheless this fact alone stands in the favour of Zeppelins, in that fateful year of 1937. A similar accident in any other type of aircraft would almost certainly have killed all on board.

The Second World War found both the LZ-127 *Graf Zeppelin* and the new LZ-130 suspended in their sheds at Frankfurt, awaiting supplies of helium from America. On 20 February 1940, Goering, Commander in Chief of the *Luftwaffe*, ordered the destruction of both airships on the grounds that their material was wanted for the building of *Luftwaffe* aircraft. Later the *Luftwaffe* demolished both sheds because they were: 'blocking the take-off path of *Luftwaffe* bombers during the battle of France.'

Fifty years on, with hindsight, it can be recognised that the aeroplane would overtake the airship for airline work. Between the wars this was not the case. Zeppelins, manned by superbly trained airshipmen, pioneered the way all across the world, setting standards and procedures of airmanship which went a long way in establishing present-day air transport.

An interesting point to note: the LZ-130, which did fly a number of flights over and around Germany prior to the outbreak of the Second World War, is often referred to as *Graf Zeppelin 2*. This is incorrect, the LZ-130 was never officially christened.

CHAPTER EIGHT

Triumph and Tragedy in the Arctic

Italy played a vital part in airship history. Throughout the First World War her airshipmen carried out many bombing missions on the Italian fronts. Italians developed the semi-rigid airship, that is, a large envelope containing hydrogen with balancing ballonets, plus a rigid keel which effectively went from nose to tail. This framework, of triangular form, was attached to the base of the envelope and it contained the control-car and bomb-load etc., terminating in the tail surfaces. Engine-cars were also fixed to this triangular keel. Viewed head-on, the profile of envelope plus large triangular keel appears pear-shaped. Italy operated a rudimentary commercial airship service between Milan and Venice in 1919 using two 20-seater modified military airships. It was not a success.

The prominent Italian airship designer Col Umberto Nobile, built in 1923 for the Italian Government, the first of the N-class semi-rigids, N-1. N-1 was 348 ft long with a capacity of 550,00 cu ft. Three 250-hp Fiat engines gave a maximum speed of 71.4 mph. An economical 50 mph was possible using only two engines. Half as big again as the British wartime North Sea class, which was arguably the finest non-rigid airship of its day, the N-1 was a very efficient airship.

Umberto Nobile studied at the Naples Polytechnic, qualifying with great distinction. In 1912, after working for the State railways in a technical capacity, he began studying aeronautical engineering with special attention to airships. When Italy entered the First World War, he offered his services to the Italian War Ministry. Consequently he became the vice-director of the airship branch of the Italian Air Service.

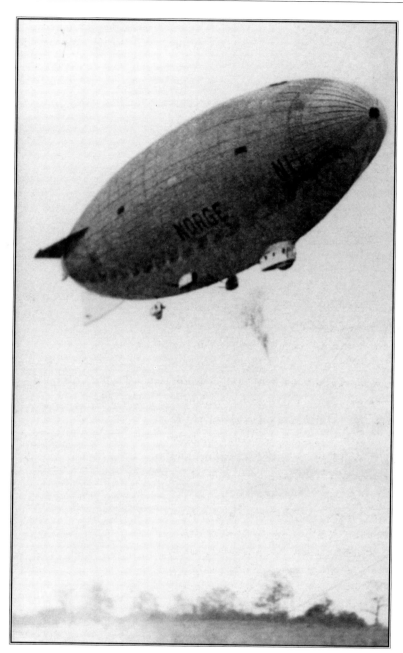

The Italian airship N.1 *Norge* landing at RAF Pulham on 11 April 1926, en route for Spitzbergen and her successful trans-polar flight. The 'pear-shaped' head-on profile which most semi-rigid airships acquired is apparent in this picture. The 'cloud' beneath her is water ballast which has just been dropped to assist the landing. (*David Cook via Ces Mowthorpe Collection*)

It was here that his influence on the semi-rigid type of airship enhanced its efficiency, so much so that Great Britain bought one of his latest 'M' type and flew it, in October 1918, from Rome to Pulham, England. Under Capt George Meager, with Capt T.B. Williams as his second officer, and an all-British crew (every one, ex-

RNAS and now RAF, experienced airshipmen), this airship, officially numbered by the RAF as the SR-1, made the journey, with two refuelling stops at French airship bases, in three and a half days. This was a record flight for those days and created several records, and, alone, proved the efficiency of Nobile's design. Further examples were bought by Spain and the Argentine Republic. Hence his post-war design, the 'N' class was in every respect at the forefront of non-rigid airship design. Remember, in 1924 no one had flown over the North Pole. It had never been mapped, and no civilisation existed between Spitzbergen to the east and Alaska/Siberia to the west — 2,300 miles of uncharted wasteland, subjected to violent weather patterns. Ordinary compasses were useless owing to large, unknown magnetic variations and radio reception was dubious, to say the least.

Roald Amundsen, the famous Antarctic explorer had attempted to fly over the Pole with two Dornier seaplanes in the Spring of 1925. Forced to crash-land on the ice, he and his four companions endured twenty-five days of extreme hardship until, by a remarkable feat of airmanship, one of the planes was able to take off and bring them to safety. Although fifty-three years old, Amundsen prepared for another such flight. He was backed financially by the American Lincoln Ellsworth and they decided an airship was the only vehicle capable of achieving this notable flight. A fellow Norwegian and pilot of one of the Dorniers, Riiser-Larsen, had been trained in Britain as an airship pilot and it was he who recommended that the Italian airship N-1 would be an ideal craft.

Mussolini agreed to sell the ship for 75,000 dollars and Nobile agreed to pilot it with an Italian crew. It was basically a Norwegian–American venture, using an Italian airship and crew, but friction between Amundsen and Nobile was sure to erupt due to wildly differing personalities. Nobile was the airship captain but Amundsen insisted upon complete control, regarding Nobile merely as 'the hired pilot'. Despite these obvious problems, mutual admiration enabled the venture to go ahead.

Amundsen's aeroplane flight had started from King's Bay, Spitzbergen and it was here that the Norwegian Aero Club (under whose supervision the flight was undertaken), built an ingenious roofless airship shed. Constructed specially for the N-1, now officially christened the *Norge*, it was open-ended but when one walked inside the airship, it offered excellent base facilities in bad weather. A small mooring-mast was also available.

Overhauled and modified for the polar flight, *Norge* left her Italian base at Campino on 10 April 1926 *en route* for Pulham, England. Spending two nights here, *Norge* lifted off on her next stage to Gatchina, near Leningrad on 14 April. Here, final preparations were carried out while awaiting confirmation that King's Bay was ready. On the 5 May *Norge* ascended and set course for Spitzbergen where she was safely berthed in her roofless shed 39 hrs later, despite one of the motors being disabled. Her mixed crew of Norwegian and Italians, plus one Swede, worked well together as a team. Though her polar flight proper had not begun, *Norge* had already accomplished a remarkable flight, from the semi-tropical Mediterranean up to the most northerly airfield in the world, without a serious hitch.

A new motor was fitted from supplies brought by sea to King's Bay, and finally, at 0830 hrs on 11 May 1926, the *Norge* rose slowly into the northern sky. In command was Amundsen, who gave orders to Nobile and his crew. Accompanying Nobile was a pet terrier, Titania, his constant companion. Sixteen men made the flight, seven, including Amundsen were Norwegians, one at each of the rudder and elevator controls, Riiser-Larsen was the navigator and Birger Gottwaldt and Storm-Johnsen manned the radio while a Norwegian journalist Ramm scribbled dispatches for relay to King's Bay. A Swedish aerologist or weatherman, was Finn Malmgren, Nobile and the Italians formed the remainder plus the American Ellsworth whom assisted with the navigation. Despite obvious language difficulties the mixed crew worked well together.

A high-pressure weather system prevailed over the North Pole and the *Norge* flew steadily northwards, mostly in a freezing fog which encrusted her exterior with ice. As the distance towards the Pole decreased, so the compasses became more erratic. Nobile frequently took his ship up to 3,000 ft, breaking through into the Arctic sunshine, thus thawing the encrusted ice and enabling Riisen-Larsen to get accurate position fixes using the sun compass. Sun compasses require concentration, keeping their artificial horizon level with the horizon proper. Riisen-Larsen was so engrossed that on one occasion the *Norge* flew a complete circle before resuming the correct course.

At 0130 hrs on the 12 May 1926 *Norge* crossed over the North Pole in fine weather. Nobile circled the Pole, weighted national flags were thrown overboard and the Norwegian, American and Italian flags fluttered bravely onto the snow below. The worst part of the flight was to follow. Completely unexplored territory lay between the *Norge* and Alaska where she hoped to land at Nome on Point Barrow.

Fog again enveloped the ship and although the magnetic compasses were now becoming operative, navigation was difficult. Ice formed everywhere, the radio aerial encased so badly that the radio ceased to function. *Norge* was cut off from the rest of the world. Ice flew off the revolving propellers and cut deep into the keel, even penetrating the gasbag occasionally – thus requiring riggers to be extra vigilant in repairing tears with patches. Nobile came down low whenever visibility improved but the broken ice-floes showed no signs of life. Seals, birds and whales could not be seen. Early on the morning of 13 May the sun broke through, enough for Riisen-Larsen to get a firm fix. He calculated that they should strike the Alaskan coastline at about 0800 hrs. By 0725 hrs, the *Norge* was again over land, 46 hours and 20 minutes after leaving King's Bay. The first trans-polar flight in history had been accomplished: but their ordeal was not over yet. A strong gale blew up from the Bering Straits and *Norge* became entrapped in a ravine while threading her way through the Alaskan mountain range. Slowly, so slowly, the ship made headway.

At 0130 hrs on 14 May, radio signals were heard from Nome but *Norge* was unable to reply. Eventually a river appeared below which Amundsen recognised as the Serpentine and now it was simply a matter of following the coastline. Snow squalls buffeted the airship and its fatigued crew. Nerves were stretched to breaking point and during a break between snowstorms Nobile prepared the ship for landing. A cluster of shacks appeared below, and people ran out. Lines were dropped, instructions yelled from the control-car as gradually Nobile brought the heaving ship down to a gentle landing. He remained with Titania, at the helm, while the *Norge* gradually deflated, her crew opening all valves. It was exactly 0730 hrs on 14 May 1926.

Lost in the annals of time, this first trans-polar flight is never given the credit it deserves. A magnificent triumph for an airship – no aeroplane at that time could have accomplished the same. The mixed Norwegian/Italian crew pulled together magnificently despite language differences. Sad to relate, the world's press concentrated almost entirely upon a long-standing difference of opinion between Nobile and Amundsen. This had nothing to do with the flight itself (it was over publishing rights which Amundsen thought Nobile should not have been given), and is no part of this book about airshipmen.

Nobile received a tumultuous reception back in Italy. Now obsessed with the Arctic, and in spite of his quarrel with Amundsen, he proposed a further flight using a new airship. Amundsen curtly declined, saying that his exploring days were over. Nobile pressed on with a certain amount of encouragement from Italy's dictator, Mussolini. Inspired by Lindbergh's solo Atlantic crossing, Mussolini, eager for Italy's participation into this new air age, agreed to provide a ship and crew under the sponsorship of the Italian Royal Geographical Society and the City of Milan.

Though larger than the *Norge*, the *Italia* was of similar design, but used modern materials and weighed in nearly 3,000 lb lighter. Reinforcement to the lower envelope and keel gave protection against flying ice from the propellers, thus precluding the damage which was a serious problem with the *Norge*. Covered observation points were added so the navigators could take sun-sights without going outside the ship. Radio aerials were specially designed to be less affected by ice. It was proposed to hover over the Pole while scientists temporarily disembarked to take observations so an ingenious pneumatic-controlled winch and basket was provided. Pressure altimeters had proved unreliable in Arctic skies therefore Nobile carried glass balls filled with bright red paint. Timing the fall of these balls onto the ice, he calculated that they fell at a rate of 60 feet per second, thus providing reasonably reliable readings. From the foregoing the reader can deduce that this was not to be a 'simple' flight to the North Pole but a scientific expedition, with extended plans if possible, to map the still unknown coastlines and seas between the North Pole and Canada. King's Bay would again provide a working base for these exploratory flights.

Much detailed planning went into survival equipment in case the worst befell the expedition. This included two sledges, rifles, revolvers, snowshoes and special emergency food rations. All the crew wore special undergarments and a buttonless outer flying-suit with lambswool inside and treated skin outside. Skin shoes and reindeer leather shoes with several pairs of catskin socks were issued.

The crew was carefully chosen. Six of the *Norge*'s crew and two of Nobiles's airship building team were the nucleus. From a number of volunteer radio-men, two were chosen. Three naval officers were in charge of navigation and meterology, all possessing airship experience. Two scientists, Drs Behounek and Pontremoli were in charge of scientific experiments and data. Two Italian newspapermen made up the final total of eighteen, plus of course, Nobile's pet terrier Titania.

The flight to King's Bay, Spitzbergen was via Stolp in Germany and Vadsö in Norway. At 0155 hrs on 15 April 1928 *Italia* departed her Milan base. Weather deteriorated and as the ship crossed the Alpine range, it got worse. The port fin was damaged while passing Trieste and an electrical storm of great magnitude compelled Nobile to risk flying through passes to avoid rising above pressure height. Hailstones on the envelope added greatly to her weight but gradually, by brilliant helmsmanship Nobile broke through to the Germanic plains, arriving over Stolp at 0750 hrs. Such had been the struggle to survive that not a pound of ballast remained on board. The upper fin was fractured and all three propellers severely pitted by hailstones. Few, if any airships had survived under such conditions. *Italia*'s strength was proven, as indeed, was the Nobile's airmanship.

Owing to the late arrival of supplies at King's Bay, departure from Stolp was delayed, *Italia* eventually mooring to King's Bay mast at 0855 hrs on 4 May. But the weather had worsened, and such was the blizzard that Nobile ordered a skeleton crew to man the ship. Two engines were started and using these to keep 'head to wind', disaster was averted.

Gradually snow turned to rain, thus after consultation, with a full crew, Nobile cast off for the Arctic at 0530 a.m. Fighting 45-mph winds, *Italia* flew up Spitzbergen's uncharted western coastline, when after several hours one of the engines failed. Prudently, Nobile steered back to King's Bay, landing at the mast at 1245 p.m. the same day. With a rising wind, Nobile requested assistance from the crew of the Italian supply ship *City of Milan*, to control the heaving airship. His request was refused. For the first time, Nobile, pioneer airship builder and pilot, realised he had political enemies. Thankfully, an emergency call to the residents of the nearby mining town of Ny Aalesund averted disaster. Two hundred men arrived after four hours. During a lull in the wind, *Italia* was safely docked inside the shed.

Four days later, a replacement engine fitted and the ship overhauled, *Italia* departed for a survey flight to Nicholas II land at 0800 hrs on 11 May 1928. A fierce gale blew up and due to bad visibility in the blizzard, the scientists could accomplish nought. Again, a return to base was achieved after only eight hours flying. On this flight Nobile was stunned when shown a severely frayed control wire. As he had personally inspected all the control wires while *Italia* was laid up in the shed, he was convinced it was sabotage. Meanwhile, foreign newspaper men at King's Bay were sending disparaging reports about the failure of *Italia* to finish either

Italia approaches the mast at King's Bay, Spitzbergen. (*Ces Mowthorpe Collection*)

of the two flights on which she had set out. No mention was made of the adverse weather and brilliant airmanship of commander and crew. Severe snow-storms while in the roofless hangar meant the envelope of the ship had to be continually swept to keep the weight of snow down. The same newspaper men who had praised this innovative hangar when it was built two years previously by the Norwegians, now ridiculed the 'airship shed with no roof'.

During the afternoon of 15 May *Italia* took off on another attempt to overfly Nicholas II Land. Carrying much scientific equipment, thirteen crew members, two scientists and a journalist, she headed north. Passing Cape North, bad weather was encountered though visibility remained good. Flying further and further into unexplored territory the airship encountered only odd polar bears and arctic seabirds – all scattering at the approach of this noisy intruder. Several times land appeared on the horizon, then rapidly disappeared – Nobile soon realised these were mirages, brought about by the refraction of light on the ice. After a day and a half no sign of land was found. Certainly Gillis Land, as shown on all maps, either did not exist or was in some other position. Over 60,000 of previously uncharted square miles was covered and surveyed from the air. Retracing her outward flight, *Italia* landed at King's Bay on 18 May after a successful 69-hour flight. Again the newsmen at the base were dissatisfied. With no spectacular occasions such as landing at the Pole or similar, the scientific and surveying accomplishments were overlooked. Disparaging reports were sent back to the world's press.

The ingenious roofless airship shed built at King's Bay, Spitzbergen, and used by the two Italian semi-rigids *Norge* and *Italia*. Praised by the world's press as a brilliant conception when built, the same pressmen ridiculed the design during *Italia*'s occupation. (*Ces Mowthorpe Collection*)

Preparing for a flight to the Pole on 22 May, Nobile personally toured his craft examining and testing all equipment. In the tail portion he discovered a small tear in the envelope from which hydrogen was escaping. This seemed to have been done deliberately with a knife, but could not be proven. A patch was placed over the slit but this incident troubled Nobile greatly. He became more and more convinced that someone in his crew was committing sabotage.

A pre-flight champagne party was laid on, the expeditions padre blessing the flight. At 0428 hrs, *Italia* rose into the afternoon sky while a drunken brawl broke out among the newspapermen below. Sixteen souls were aboard plus the little dog, Titania.

By 0600 hrs they were crossing the ice-pack; twelve hours later at 1800 hrs they were a few miles off Cape Bridgeman on Greenland's coast. Their course was to the west of *Norge*'s track of two years previously, over unmapped territory, but fine weather and 60-mile visibility around the airship promised well. Nearing the Pole *Italia* was flying with a substantial tailwind. Nobile had much discussion with his navigator Malmgren about carrying straight on to Alaska after passing the Pole. However, Malmgren persuaded his captain to return to King's Bay and make a further flight over the Arctic. Nobile expressed doubts about fighting what would become a strong head-wind if they turned back. Malmgren was convinced the wind would drop. Nobile then made the fateful decision to return to King's Bay.

Passing through a storm the ship emerged into clear skies 50 miles prior to reaching her goal. At 0120 hrs on the morning of 24 May, Nobile slowed engines after circling the Pole and dropped the Italian flag, and a crucifix from the people of Forli, Milan, who had requested such a gesture. Head to wind and almost stationary, prayers were said while the portable gramophone played softly. Malmgren turned to Nobile and quietly remarked 'Few men can say they have been to the North Pole twice, as we can.' Sadly the wind was too strong to permit a landing in any form but this in no way detracted from the achievement. Pontremoli, the senior scientist excitedly came up to Nobile and shouted that he had measured the horizontal component of the terrestrial magnetic field of the Pole – a calculation never possible before. Nobile smiled and passed around his silver flask filled with egg-nog. Telegrams were sent by radio to the Pope, the King and Mussolini.

Opening out the motors, *Italia* turned on to a reciprocal course, heading back to base. For 24 hours she flew steadily into an increasing head-wind. The crew, now suffering from fatigue, silently became aware that they were moving ever slower across the forbidding icefield. The temperature dropped alarmingly, ice covered the struggling airship and all radio contact was lost. So far, *Italia* had cruised on two motors only, her most economical state. Now, in order to get through to better weather beyond, Nobile ordered the third motor to be started but their groudspeed scarcely increased. Full power made little difference and fearful of straining his struggling craft, Nobile ordered power to be reduced. All day the ship fought her way over the ice at 500 ft but no hole in the storm could be found. Uncertain of his position, Nobile finally got through to the support ship *City of Milan* at King's Bay. Garbled messages gave uncertain directions and lowering cloud made solar observations impossible.

At 0925 on 25 May, Nobile was in the radio-shack when the elevator helmsman, Trojani, shouted out that the elevators had jammed solid. Nobile rushed forward to assist but the wheel refused to budge. Engines were stopped and ballast discharged. Slowly, the airship rose out of the cloud into sunlight at 3,000 ft. Now the elevator worked normally, it had frozen solid in the freezing cloud below. Solar shots were taken and it was estimated that King's Bay was about six hours flying time away – if all went well.

Having burned her original fuel load and discharged ballast, *Italia* was now very light. In order to maintain a steady 300 ft, the nose was permanently tilted down. Nobile was busy taking altitude measurements in the nose of the gondola when the helmsman shouted, 'We're heavy.' Startled, Nobile took over the control and was amazed to see that although the nose was pointing up, the ship was descending. Ordering full power to lift the nose Nobile's eyes stared at the variometer. It was still dropping. Knowing now that a crash was imminent he swiftly shut all motors down to lessen the impact. The stern struck first, then the control-car crashed violently into the icepack.

The control-car broke away from the airship, which thus lightened, lifted off the ice and was swept away, never to be seen again. Six souls were still on board. The remainder, some with broken limbs, collected as much equipment and rations that they could find, including the emergency battery-driven radio and made a makeshift camp on the frozen ice.

Meanwhile in Italy, celebrations were afoot after receiving the message that *Italia* had reached the Pole. With the cessation of radio signals on 25 May, however, all those concerned with the flight realised that an emergency had occurred. Two days later, serious attempts to form a rescue expedition took place. Roald Amundsen, despite his long-standing disagreement with Nobile, immediately volunteered his services. These were accepted and the expedition set forth a few days later. Sad to relate, this expedition lost contact with its base and was never heard of again.

It is not the task of this book to enumerate the horrific trials Nobile and the remainder of his crew suffered over the next twenty-five days. Contact by radio was established, then lost. The survivors' position was never really certain to the rescue teams. Finally on 19 June they sighted an aircraft. Two days later, two aeroplanes discovered them and dropped supplies. More followed. Four days later a light aeroplane equipped with skis managed to land close by. After thirty-one days on the ice help was at hand. By general consensus of the survivors, Nobile (and his dog) were taken out with the first group. Nobile was chosen because he was the best person to organise further airlifts. Sadly, for various reasons, mostly political, it was a further fortnight before the remaining survivors were lifted off. Nothing was ever heard again of the Amundsen expedition, the six *Italia* crew members seen drifting away in the stricken airship, and two Russian airmen who disappeared while searching for Nobile. They were lost forever in the Arctic wastes.

Nobile was reviled by the world press, accused of 'deserting his companions', causing trouble with the search team and receiving every possible insult that could be fabricated. In Italy, Nobile and the survivors received a triumphant reception but slowly the Fascist government turned the screws and on 3 March 1929 they publicly denounced him, stripping him of all rank. A full report by the Italian government published in February 1930 cast reflections both on his technical qualities 'as a pilot' and upon his capacity for command. His reputation in tatters, Nobile never received the respect that his achievements deserved. Russia employed him as

General Umberto Nobile and his pet terrier, Titania, pose in the doorway of the *Italia* in April 1929. (*Ces Mowthorpe Collection*)

——————————— successful track of *Norge*, May 1926
- - - - - - - - - - - - - - final flight of *Italia*, May 1928

Although well publicised at the time, the world today has largely forgotten the outstanding work done by those two magnificent Italian airships, *Norge* and *Italia*, together with their gallant crews.

Deputy Chief of Airship Construction during the 1930s to design and build at least one large semi-rigid ship. Returning to his native Italy after the Fascist regime foundered, he died on 29 July 1978, aged ninety-three years.

Sixty years after the ill-fated flight of the *Italia*, the true facts about this gallant airshipman's triumphs were acknowledged and he was publicly reinstated, complete with his decorations.

Although well publicised at the time, the world today has largely forgotten the outstanding work done by those two magnificent Italian airships *Norge* and *Italia*, together with their gallant crews.

CHAPTER NINE

American Airshipmen

arlier pages showed that adventurous young Americans had imitated Santos-Dumont and built small airships purely for sporting reasons, but the American Army and Navy were not interested in lighter-than-air craft, though some interest had been shown in aeroplanes. The First World War changed everything. Widely reported 'successes' – greatly exaggerated – of the German Zeppelin and the positive successes of the German U-boats, convinced the US Navy that airships, on the lines of the British SS-ships should be developed. The first American Naval airship, the DN-1 (Dirigible Non-rigid No. 1) was launched in 1917. Built and flown at Pensacola, Florida, it was not really suitable. After a few flights it was discreetly dismantled.

Several American 'observers' serving with the Royal Navy reported upon the ingenious mating of an aeroplane fuselage to an envelope that had produced the SS-class non-rigid 'blimps', suitable for U-boat patrol work. Immediate steps were taken in Washington to emulate the British. The Goodyear Tyre and Rubber company had slight aeronautical experience and they were awarded a contract for nine of the projected 'B-class' non-rigids. Ordered off the drawing-board, sixteen were finally operational. Not only did Goodyear build the airships, they undertook full responsibility for training all crews. The first contingent began training at Akron, Ohio in October 1917. Their senior officer was Lt Maxfield, later to lose his life over the River Humber, England, in the ill-fated R-38 which the British had sold to the Americans as the ZR-2. Some of these 'Naval aviators (Dirigible)' – to give them their correct name – were sent to France after completing their training at Akron to gain experience with the French naval airship. Later trainees were also sent to Britain and flew with RNAS airships.

On 1 March 1918 the US Navy purchased a French non-rigid airship, the AT-13. This airship had already seen service with the

French Navy but made her first American patrol under the command of Lt Maxfield from Paimboeuf on 3 March. The patrol of 1 October the same year was an interesting one for AT-13 and her American crew. While escorting a convoy the opportunity was taken to fire the nose-mounted cannon (a feature of some French airships). Carefully aiming at a convenient exposed rock, the gun-layer pressed the trigger. After the second shot the gun stopped with a broken firing-pin, thus rendering the airship defenceless, except for her bombs. Circling around the convoy in the late afternoon, Lt Maxfield spotted a submarine, which, instead of diving, opened fire on the airship with her 4-inch deck gun. Thirteen shells exploded around the AT-13 but fortunately no harm was done. Still giving chase, the airship was unable to overtake the submarine and drop bombs. Calling up escorts, Lt Maxfield continued to shadow his adversary but eventually lost contact in the evening gloom. Despite an inconclusive end to the encounter, the submarine was deflected from its task of attacking the convoy. Thus Lt Maxfield and his crew became the first American airshipmen to meet a fighting adversary. They rose to the challenge admirably.

In England, the US Navy purchased one of the modern Zero-class non-rigids. This was placed under the command of Ensign Phil Barnes whose crew were an American engineer and wireless operator. A ground crew of American naval personnel (collectively these are recorded as 'The American Contingent') serviced their SSZ-23. Stationed at RNAS Howden in East Yorkshire, numerous war patrols were carried out over the North Sea. Seconded to the Howden sub-station of Lowthorpe during early spring-time, when the airfield was covered in buttercups, Ensign Barnes was so impressed that he immediately wrote home to his parents that he had 'landed on a field of gold!'

Later in the year this US Naval presence at RNAS Howden was increased to four Zero crews under Ensigns Pete Wolf, Harrison Goodspeed and Pope. On 29/30 May 1918, Ensign Barnes (soon to be promoted to lieutenant on his 21st birthday) accomplished a flight of 25 hrs in his SSZ-23, which created a record for Zero-class airships that was not broken until after hostilities ceased.

Meanwhile across the Atlantic, the B-class American blimp, with its 84,000-cu ft envelope and two air ballonets, inflated via the propeller slipstream, similar to the British method, started operations. An endurance of twelve hours was planned. Although

The record-breaking American Coastal airship C.5 landing at Newfoundland on 14 May 1919 after her record non-stop flight from Cape May. Refuelled and prepared for a transatlantic crossing on 17 May (it would have been the first crossing by any aircraft), she was lost at her moorings in a sudden gale on the night of 15/16 May 1919. (*JMB/GSL Collection*)

specially built, the gondola or control-car was on the lines of an aeroplane fuselage with three cockpits. Radio was carried and there was a single engine up front, driving a tractor propeller.

Duties consisted of anti-submarine patrols from American east coast bases, escorting convoys and photograhic missions. By the end of hostilities these sixteen airships had flown over 13,000 hrs on operations. Like their British equivalents, their task was not to destroy U-boats, but to discourage U-boat attacks in their vicinity. The assumption was that attacking U-boat captains would expect to be spotted from the track of their torpedoes and come under immediate attack themselves from the escorts, summoned by the airship's radio. American airship pilots called these B-ships 'pony-blimps', a nickname they carried over to the British Zeros, which some of them later flew.

During 1918 the American Navy designed and built thirteen C-class twin-engined non-rigids. These were of their own design and owed little to outside influence. Twin-engined (two 150-hp Hispanos or two 120-hp Unions turning pusher propellers), with a 181,000-cu ft envelope. These were very practical aircraft capable of 48-hr patrols (2,100 miles at cruising speed 45 mph) with a crew of five or six. Maximum speed was 60 mph. Production was meant to be over a hundred but by the time hostilities had ceased in November 1918, only ten were built, six by Goodyear and four by the Goodrich Company. Often referred to as 'Coastals' by their crews, these must not be confused with the British 'Coastal' which was a much earlier airship.

By 1919, airmen on both sides of the Atlantic had set their sights on the first Atlantic crossing by air. Competition was keen between the American naval airmen flying aeroplanes and their compatriots flying airships. Both branches were trying to outdo the other. Lt Cdr Read set out with three Curtiss flying-boats on 8 May 1919 crossing via the Azores. Only one flying-boat succeeded, arriving at Plymouth, England, on 31 May. They nearly lost this achievement to the lighter-than-air boys.

C.5 made a record-breaking non-stop flight for any aircraft, from Cape May to Newfoundland, staging through Nantucket on 14 May 1919. Refuelled and with a rested crew, C.5 was all prepared to make a direct non-stop flight to England on 17 May which should have accomplished the Atlantic crossing before the Curtiss flying-boats. Sadly on the night of the 15/16 May a strong gale suddenly whipped up tearing the airship from her moorings, totally destroying her. Thus ended a valiant effort by American naval airshipmen to be the 'first across'.

A further record held by these C-class ships was with C.7. In December 1921, C.7 was inflated with helium, the first operational airship in the world to fly with this non-inflammable gas. Experiments with C.7 ensured that the huge airship programmes, later carried out

An American Coastal-class non-rigid on patrol in 1918. These American airships are not to be confused with the British Coastal-class which were slightly smaller, with an engine at both ends of the car. The American Coastal had its two engines mounted on gantrys, above and forward, on the car. (*JMB/GSL Collection*)

by the Americans, never suffered the tragic fate of so many hydrogen-filled airships. It should be understood that in the 1920s, America was the only country in the world with enough helium (in America, a natural gas, but expensive to extract) for inflating airships.

America's first commercial airship named *Wingfoot Express*, was built by Goodyear in 1919. An experimental airship, 162 ft long, with a gas capacity of 200,000 cu ft, it was intended to carry eight fare-paying passengers. To save weight, two 80-hp rotary aeroplane engines were fitted. These rotaries – where the propeller was bolted to the cylinders which rotated around a stationary crankshaft, had been successfully used by aircraft during the First World War. Cooling was effected by the speedy rotation of the cylinders, thus doing away with a weighty cooling system. However, hot exhaust gasses were ejected direct from the exhaust valve in the cylinder head and swept into the slipstream. Not a brilliant idea in the proximity of thousands of cubic feet of hydrogen.

Wingfoot Express was assembled and flown from the White City Park hangar, in Chicago. Two experienced ex-naval airship pilots, Henry Wacker and his assistant Jack Boettner, with Buck Weaver as engineer, made two short trials flights in July 1919 from White City. On 21 July 1919, with two passengers, one a newspaper reporter, the airship took off on a promotional flight over Chicago. All wore parachutes.

Meanwhile Chicago was going about its daily business. The huge glass-roofed Illinois Trust and Savings Bank was packed with 200

The *Wingfoot Express* lifting off from White City Park, Chicago, on 22 July 1919. The pilot, who was saved by his parachute, was Jack Boettner, and later became the Chief Pilot of the Goodyear Fleet of civilian airships. Boettner and Henry Wacker, the only survivors, became the first members of the 'Caterpillar Club' aircrew whose lives had been saved, by in this case, Spencer Parachutes. (*Ces Mowthorpe Collection*)

staff and customers. Suddenly the *Wingfoot Express* was seen to burst into flames at 500 ft, and fall from the sky. At the last minute three parachutes were seen to open, sadly one was overtaken by the burning wreckage but the other two landed safely. Inside the bank everyone was startled by a body falling through the glass roof followed instantly by two blazing petrol tanks and the flaming wreckage. Three of the people in the airship and nine members of the bank staff perished. Twenty-seven others were seriously injured. One saved by parachute was the assistant pilot Jack Boettner (later to command the Goodyear blimp fleet in the 1940s). His opinion was that the two rotary engines had been situated too close to the envelope, being mounted higher than the gondola. Hence sparks from the rotating exhaust valves had set fire to outer cover. A tragedy indeed.

On 21 February 1922 the US Army's Italian designed semi-rigid airship *Roma* burst into flames killing thirty-four of the forty-five men on board. The result of these two disasters, plus the loss of the British-built ZR-2 (R.38) over the River Humber, England in 1921 with the loss of American lives, turned the American people, and especially Congress, against hydrogen-filled airships. The bold and expensive ($120 per 1,000 cu ft in 1922) decision to use helium, with only 92 per cent of the lifting power of hydrogen was far-reaching but no doubt saved many airshipmen's lives. It did however, due to the reluctance to vent the expensive helium, contribute to the loss of the ZR-1, *Shenandoah*.

The reader may at this point ponder on the apparent fascination with airships. Reading about the loss of life and material – as well as the remarkable escapes – begs the question, 'Why bother with airships?' By the end of the First World War air power was established. The aeroplane had come to stay. However, it was not (in the 1920s) a great weight lifter. Likewise if the engine(s) stopped, it would descend to earth very quickly, often with fatal results. Whereas the airship, supported by its lifting gas, carried much more, much further and if engines stopped, could float gently to earth. It was the only true long-range transcontinental machine available. After the wartime successes of the German Zeppelins it appeared well worth encouraging.

America had long coastlines on two oceans with particular need of long-distance airborne maritime reconnaissance for its Fleet. Initially two large rigid airships would be aquired, one built in America (ZR-1 *Shenandoah*) and one bought from abroad. They wished to buy a modern Zeppelin but the Armistice terms forbade Germany building or selling any airship. Great Britain, the second largest builder of rigid airships, had proved her ability with the transatlantic double flight of the R.34 in 1919 (albeit a copy of the German 30-class Zeppelin). Hence the decision made to buy from Britain the still-to-be-completed R.38 (ZR-2). Sadly, as we have seen, this airship broke up in the air over the River Humber during trials, with the loss of forty-four souls, sixteen of them American. As a direct result of this unfortunate catastrophe, America persuaded the Allied Commission to allow the Zeppelin Company to build the second rigid. America also pointed out that compensation was due for the two airships America should have received but did not, due to the scuttling of Zeppelins by the German navy. This resulted in the German-built Zeppelin, designated LZ-126, and later christened *Los Angeles*. She was filled with hydrogen initially, for her trials and transatlantic delivery flight. This hydrogen was later discharged when she reached her shed at Lakehurst, New Jersey, USA and replaced by helium.

As previously stated, helium was still rare and expensive. Consequently, in order to conserve helium, the US Navy developed a policy of 'flying the ship heavy'. This meant maintaining altitude below pressure height by use of elevators and motors – an accepted method, but not used for extended periods by the Germans and the British, who simply valved the cheaper hydrogen and dropped ballast to lighten the ship later. The last captain of *Shenandoah*, Lt Cdr Zachary Lansdowne, a highly competent airshipman who served with the RNAS in Britain during the First World War, was especially conscious of the necessity for conserving the expensive helium. An excellent airshipman, he devised several 'unorthodox' methods to achieve his aim. His most controversial action, which was subsequently to be held partially responsible for *Shenandoah*'s tragic demise on 3 September 1925, was taken during her extensive overhaul at Lakehurst in early 1925.

Shenandoah had eighteen automatic valves at the base of her gas-cells, discharging into trunks which carried the gas out through vents at the top of the hull. She also had sixteen manoeuvring valves at the top of gas-cells which were operated by cables in the control-car. Any valves, however well fitted, are never completely gas-tight. Cdr Lansdowne had eight manoeuvring valves removed and then ten of the automatics, together with their trunking. He also insisted that whenever *Shenandoah* was in her shed, self-sealing 'jam-pot' covers were placed over the automatic valves. It became standard practice to fly with these 'jam-pots' and if or when the ship reached pressure height, riggers swiftly removed them.

This was the state of the airship when *Shenandoah*, without warning, entered an area of extreme atmospheric instability, loosely called a line squall, on 3 September 1925, over Ohio. A violent rise to 6,000 ft was followed by a sudden drop to 3,000 ft when she started rising again. The tortured hull could stand no more, and broke at frame 125. Tied together temporarily by the control cables, she rose swiftly. The control-car broke free plunging earthwards with its six occupants. A further break in the after portion occurred at frame 110, hurling engine cars and their mechanics to the ground. Now in three pieces, the stricken ship drifted with the wind. The navigating officer, Lt Cdr Rosendahl and six crewmen safely ballooned to earth. Dropping slowly, the tail section also brought its occupants safely down. Twenty-nine out of the forty-four airshipmen survived thanks to the use of helium. Among those who died was her captain, Cdr Lansdowne. The question is, would *Shenandoah* have weathered the storm if conservation of this expensive gas had not been so vital?

When the Zeppelin company at Freidrichshafen got permission to build a Zeppelin for the American navy in December 1921, they firmly believed that this would be the last Zeppelin built by them. Ignoring the fact that America had been on the side of the Allies during the recent conflict, German/American relations were generally good. These two points compelled the German company to

The tail section of *Shenandoah* where it fell at Ava, Ohio, on 3 September 1925. After breaking into three sections, this helium-filled rigid saved 29 souls, mostly in the middle and tail sections which floated safely to the ground. (*Ces Mowthorpe Collection*)

excel in their commission. LZ-126 incorporated every known modification that four years of wartime experience with over one hundred similar ships could provide. Larger and more streamlined, with a single spacious gondola firmly attached to the hull, this superb craft was powered by five modern Maybach engines.

On 15 October 1924, LZ-126 arrived safely at Lakehurst after an 81½-hour flight from southern Germany. On entering the Lakehurst shed, she officially became the property of the US Navy being christened ZR-3 *Los Angeles*. Immediately shedded, she was drained of hydrogen and refilled with helium from the ZR-1 *Shenandoah* berthed alongside. The sheer expense of helium inflation prompted the US Navy to keep only one rigid at flight status during these early years. ZR-3 *Los Angeles* served her new masters well for fourteen years. Finally, in 1938 she was pronounced as uneconomical and reduced to scrap in 1939. During her long career she flew thousands of miles in all weathers and never lost an airshipman's life.

A remarkable incident occurred to *Los Angeles*, on 25 August 1927 at 1329 hrs, unique in airship records. Swinging gently at Lakehurst's high mooring-mast, the ship was overtaken by a cold front advancing from the sea. Cold air pressure lifted the stern higher and higher until *Los Angeles* was almost vertical to the mast. Inside the ship the mast-watch crew hung on for their dear lives. Mess gear and provisions slid down into the bows of the ship, falling tools and spares followed. Fortunately, petrol and water ballast held fast although some water did trickle through into the control room. Lt 'Tex' Settle, officer-in-charge, wedged himself against the rudder-wheel and anxiously watched the ground appearing between his knees, 200 ft below. For several minutes, *Los Angeles* pirouetted like a ballerina on top of the mast. Then, turning through ninety degrees, her stern slowly descended into its proper position and apart from the mess in the bows, things returned to normal. The whole sequence took about six minutes while the whole station looked on – none more anxiously than her captain, Cdr Rosendahl. Six photographs of this phenomenon were taken by the Navy. For fear of an outburst of public opinion against the rigid airship, they were not released for another thirty years. As a direct result of this incident US Navy airshipmen discontinued using the high mooring-mast, developing instead the low mooring-mast.

Los Angeles success and the general need for long-range surveillance, prompted the US Navy to propose a large rigid airship programme. Two super rigids, capable of carrying scouting aeroplanes were planned.

To meet this challenge the Goodyear Tyre and Rubber Company arranged a partnership with the German Luftschiffbau- Zeppelin Company, forming the Goodyear- Zeppelin Corporation. This effectively brought all the expertise of the German Zeppelins into the already experienced Goodyear Company in 1924. All Zeppelin patent rights and many personnel were included in this deal.

When the US Navy's Five-Year Aircraft Plan evolved in 1926, provision was made for two rigid airships. On 6 October 1928 contracts were exchanged for the building of two 6,500,000-cu ft craft. Goodyear Zeppelin built its own 'air-dock' at Akron in the hope of laying the foundation of an airship industry. This 'air-dock' was at the time of building, the largest self-supporting structure in the world, with 'orange-peel' doors. So large was the air-dock, that in humid weather, clouds could be seen forming inside the structure, under certain conditions!

These two sister-ships were the products of the foremost airship designers of the day and incorporated several innovative features. The frames and longitudinals were strong enough not to require internal wire bracing. They were built upon three keels, one at the top of the ship, two others one-third above the bottom of the hull on either side. The gas-cells were in the upper two-thirds of the hull leaving all the bottom third available for crews quarters, galley etc., eight internal engine-rooms and an aircraft hangar

25 August 1927. Owing to a peculiar weather situation, *Los Angeles* rode vertically on the high mast at Lakehurst. Fortunately, no serious damage was done although the crew on watch got quite a scare. All loose tools, or similar articles, ended up 'in the bows of the ship'. Remaining vertical for several minutes, *Los Angeles* finally settled back onto an even keel. Because of this incident – which was never reported officially, due to the fear that, coupled with the recent *Shenandoah* tragedy, American public opinion would turn against rigid airships – the American Navy stopped using high masts, concentrating upon their own superior 'low-mast' system. (*Wg Cdr Dunn via Ces Mowthorpe Collection*)

The US Navy's latest rigid, the ZR-4 *Akron*, emerges for the first time from her birthplace, the Goodyear-Zeppelin *Akron* 'air-dock', on 23 September 1931. When built between 1929 and 1930, the 'air-dock' was the largest single-structure in the world. (*Ces Mowthorpe Collection*)

containing a 'spider and trapeze' from which six small aeroplanes could be suspended. Naval designations being ZR-4 and ZR-5, they where subsequently christened *Akron* and *Macon* respectively.

With memories of the structural failures of the British-built R.38 (ZR-2) and ZR-3 *Shenandoah*, great efforts were made to prevent any structural failure. They were four times as strong as the *Shenandoah* and twice as strong as the *Los Angeles*. Work commenced in 1929, and by February 1931, ZR-3 was almost complete; then the US Navy issued Change Order No. 2, which altered the configuration of the tail fins. This change was brought about by the logical wish for the captain to be able to see his tail fin from the control-room, at all times, in order to check the trim of the ship. However, it invalidated the stress calculations which were now too low. These stresses only became obvious after flight testing and the Navy elected not to alter the design again. It was a costly decision.

Flying aeroplanes from airships was not a new idea. An Albatross fighter was dropped from the German Zeppelin L.35 in 1917 but no attempt was made to re-attach to the airship. The Royal Navy and RAF had experimented with dropping aeroplanes, Sopwith Camels and Gloucester Grebes. A De Havilland light plane successfully flew

Above: The US Army, which possessed several non-rigid airships between the two world wars, experimented with attaching aeroplanes to their airships while in flight. Here an Army Air Corps 'hooks on' to the TC-7 airship, 9 October 1925. These trials were useful forerunners for the aeroplane-carrying rigids, *Akron* and *Macon*, of later years. *Left*: Ernst Udet, well-known German First World War fighter pilot and Second World War Luftwaffe General, 'hooks on' to the LZ-129 *Hindenburg*, 11 March 1937, over Germany. This experiment was never repeated by the Germans, and the apparatus was later destroyed. The aeroplane used was a modified Focke-Wulf 44. (Above: *Goodyear Aircraft Corporation via Ces Mowthorpe Collection*. Below: *Ces Mowthorpe Collection*)

from and re-attached itself externally to the R.33. Germany's Ernst Udet successfully detached and re-attached his aeroplane to the *Hindenburg* in 1937. America had conducted many experiments with the non-rigid TC-7 in preparation for the *Akron* and *Macon*.

Akron and the *Macon*, however, had taken the great step forward to becoming virtual flying aircraft carriers. The method of detaching and retrieving their offspring was ingenious, the result of several years of experimentation using both non-rigids and the *Los Angeles*. The hangar on board was outstanding, to say the least. 75 ft long, 60 ft wide and 16 ft high. It stowed and serviced five aeroplanes. The trapeze, which was used to lower an aeroplane for dispatch and hooking returning aeroplanes on, located the aeroplanes on their X-shaped overhead trolley by means of a monorail system – all electrically operated. A further aeroplane could be suspended from the trapeze itself.

Briefly, the operation consisted of lowering the trapeze and aeroplane through a T-shaped opening in the bottom of the airship, normally covered by closed doors. When the trapeze was fully extended, about fifteen feet below the hull, the aeroplane started its motor, and flew itself off after disengaging the hook. Returning, the aeroplane, using a special attachment on its upper wing, flew onto the extended hook, stopped its engine and was retrieved through the T-shaped opening back into the hangar. Not a difficult operation for an experienced pilot. All this time the airship of course was maintaining its speed and altitude. The purpose of these aeroplanes was not to act as protection for the airship but to extend its range of surveillance. Five planes could fly out on courses ahead and abeam thus giving over a hundred miles extra scouting radius.

A two-seater naval biplane 'hooks on' to ZR-4 *Akron*, 4 May 1932. The sliding door opening above the trapeze can just be made out. (*Wg Cdr Dunn via Ces Mowthorpe Collection*)

Unfortunately, no funds were available to develop a special reconnaissance aeroplane so the Curtiss F9C – a small high-performance aircraft fighter was chosen because of its compactness. Sadly its endurance left a lot to be desired as far as the airship–aeroplane scouting concept, the very basis of the operations, was concerned. It was however, an ideal aircraft to work up squadrons for the tricky task of flying off and returning to the airship trapeze, pending a later, more suitable aeroplane.

Two other types, N2Ys and XJW-1's were individually modified. These were two/three seaters and intended to be used as 'Admiral's barges' or similar. Pilots were volunteers from the US Navy and Lt Daniel Ward, USN, undertook to 'assist in the hook-on development'. Lt Ward defined the process and wrote the Navy's manual on such operations. He went on to become the first squadron commander of the *Akron/Macon* heavier-than-air-unit: truly a unique command. He fortunately survived through being detached to other duties in late 1933.

On 5 August 1931, ZR-4 *Akron* was officially christened. The next two years saw many successful flights. However, due to operational requirements, *Akron* never flew with her complement of single-seater scouting aeroplanes. These were still in training at Lakehurst. Several two-seater aircraft were modified and at least two were always in *Akron*'s hangar. They were modified N2Ys and XJW-1's, used as utilities or in naval parlance, 'running-boats'. Without her scouting planes, ZR-4 operated with the fleet in a similar manner to that of the Zeppelins during the First World War.

On the evening of 3 April 1933, *Akron* took off on her seventy-fourth and last flight. Flying ahead of an intense cold frontal system, the ship turned out to sea to ride out the storm. Great turbulence was encountered but brilliant airmanship and use of engines enabled her to maintain her altitude of 1,600 ft. Suddenly, during a rapid descent, her tail struck the sea while her altimeter was reading 800 ft. Inclined at 45 degrees, the huge airship stalled onto the water with the loss of seventy-three souls, the executive officer Lt Cdr Wiley and two crewmen being the sole survivors.

The Court of Inquiry censured the captain, Cdr McCord, for flying too low, a sudden down-draught and faulty altimeter being contributary factors. Evidence was given by one of the survivors, Richard E. Deal, whose station was near the tail, that in the initial turbulence before the ship's final plunge, he saw the girders of the upper fin fail, with the tail girders breaking while still in flight. The weight of evidence, however, disregarded this option. Many senior airshipmen, remembering the final modification to *Akron*'s tail, placed the blame on structural failure. That *Akron* had only one rubber raft on board and no lifebelts contributed largely to the heavy loss of life.

The decision to launch ZR-5 *Macon*, almost completed at the time of *Akron*'s loss, was never in doubt. Although a sister-ship to the *Akron*, many minor modifications had been made by airshipmen in the light of experience gained with ZR-4 *Akron*. Unlike her sister-ship, *Macon*'s trapeze and aircraft hangar were fully completed and awaiting the, by now, worked-up flight of F9C single-seat scout planes.

Airshipmen wished to replace the lost *Akron* with a new rigid but now the recession was hitting America. Funding could not be found within the naval estimates. However, the *Los Angeles* was re-inflated and used – but never flown – as a ground-school ship. The whole future of American rigid lighter-than-air programmes rested upon the ZR-5 *Macon*.

ZR-5's maiden flight took place on 21 April 1933. Four further test flights took place and on 23 June, she was commissioned into the US Navy. Shortly afterwards, she set course for her station at Lakehurst, New Jersey where she arrived in the early hours of 24 June. On the 7 July 1933, *Macon* rendezvoused over New Jersey with four of her F9C aeroplanes which hooked on. American airshipmen had made history using a flying aircraft carrier, now complete, with its scouting flight.

The Chief of Naval Staff ordered *Macon* to operate on America's west coast and exercise with the Pacific Fleet. She flew from Lakehurst to her new station, Sunnyvale, in California on 12 October 1933, from where she and her aeroplanes exercised to the fullest extent in order to determine her military role.

The true role of the rigid airship aircraft carrier was for the vulnerable airship to remain hidden from view by either cloud or distance, letting her aeroplanes scout in all directions from their airborne base, reporting by radio the enemy movements. Before radar, even a vulnerable rigid airship could keep moving and thus avoid detection for many days. Her aeroplanes meanwhile providing the necessary intelligence. Due to the traditional naval distrust of flying machines in general and airships in particular ZR-5's proper potential was rarely exploited. When it was, the airship and aeroplanes more than justified their existence. Enough to say that during *Macon*'s short life, the airshipmen – and that includes the aeroplane pilots and their support – perfected countless tasks which had never been done before, and will never be done again.

A fine sight as the *Macon* sedately flies herself down to the mobile low mooring-mast. Her control-car and eight propeller-shafts can be clearly seen. These eight shafts rotated through 180 degrees so could, if required, push the airship upwards using propeller-thrust, or propel the airship backwards when turned through 180 degrees. (*Wg Cdr Dunn via Ces Mowthorpe Collection*)

It will be recalled that the amended design to the tails of both *Akron* and *Macon* required reinforcements, recommended by the designers. Due to the economic situation at that time, these reinforcements were only carried out on a temporary basis to *Macon*. No doubt when a complete overhaul became due, they would have been done. Sadly, time ran out.

On 21 April 1934 the ship was over Texas, *en route* for the Caribbean exercises. Extremely rough air was encountered and the coxswains at the wheels had to be relieved every ten minutes.

Crewmen in the keel could see the massive framework flexing in opposite directions and shortly after 1200 hrs two diagonal girders broke at frame 17.5 on the port side, damaging the main ring. Emergency repairs and reinforcements saved the ship which carried on to Opa-locka in Florida. Moored to the mast there, more permanent repairs were instituted. Returning to her base, the fin strength was thoroughly investigated and it was deemed necessary to 'strongly reinforce frame 17.5 at each of its four fin junctions'. This work was rated 'not urgent', to be carried out piecemeal during overhauls between November 1934 and February 1935. The fourth junction, that securing the upper fin to the ring never did get reinforced. It was scheduled for the March 1935 overhaul.

On the morning of 11 February, *Macon* departed Sunnyvale to 'search for all fleet units, identify them and plot their movements while her planes remained unobserved'. She exceeded all her requirements and at 1350 hrs on the 12 February was released from orders, then being at liberty to return to base.

At 1704 hrs, *Macon* was abeam the Poire Sur Light when a 'peculiar cloud condition' was seen to starboard. Capt Wiley (survivor of the *Akron* disaster) ordered 'left rudder' and the coxswain swung the wheel over. At that moment the ship was struck by a strong gust which rolled her to starboard, wrenching the wheels from both coxswains, the rudder man and elevator man. What happened next is best described by ZR-5's captain in his report:

> Immediately thereafter (the order for 'left rudder') the ship lurched suddenly as if in a powerful gust of wind, and the control wheels were spun out of the hands of both the rudderman and the elevatorman. The effect of this supposed gust was of very short duration and for a few seconds it seemed that both men on the controls had recovered control. I asked the elevatorman if his control cables were broken and he replied that he thought that he had control. Within minutes the ship began to incline up by the bow and ascend rapidly. Immediately word was given in the control-car by telephone that number one gas-cell had gone. (The US Navy followed the Zeppelin principle of numbering their gas-cells from the stern to the bows – hence number one cell was that nearest the stern.) Orders were given and executed immediately to drop all ballast and droppable fuel abaft of amidships. Engines were idled to reduce the strain on the structure of the after part of the ship and to slow the rate of rise. In spite of dropping all ballast, the inclination upward increased to at least twenty-five degrees and altitude finally reached almost 5,000 ft by altimeter. Upon receiving information that number two gas-cell was deflating I directed the radioman to send an SOS.

These gyrations were caused by failure of the still-to-be-reinforced 17.5 frame at its joint with the upper fin, puncturing cells one and two. Thus weakened, the upper fin carried away, further damaging cells 1 and 2 and rupturing cell 0 (this was right in the pointed tail of the ship).

In spite of ordering all crewmen into the bows and attempting every possible means of regaining trim *Macon* continued to descend in a nose-up attitude. At 1,700 ft, the crew were ordered to don life-jackets and prepare to abandon ship. Discipline was maintained and everyone threw out all available loose objects in order to lessen the impact when she struck the water.

At 1739 hrs her tail hit the sea and she gradually sank by the stern. The crew abandoned ship in an orderly manner, swimming to life-rafts which had been thrown overboard during the final descent. Finally sinking from view at 1820 hrs, eighty-one of her eighty-three souls on board were saved, none with serious injuries.

The loss of ZR-5 *Macon* finally convinced the US Navy that rigid airships were a luxury they could no longer afford. They did, however, agree that a small fleet of non-rigid airships should be kept 'for coastal duties'. Little did they realise how this small force would grow in the, then unforseen, Second World War.

Although the US Navy spent millions of dollars on the rigid airship programme, which it promptly shut down after the loss of the *Macon*, there was one outstanding benefit – the ground handling of airships. Even the small SS-ships of 1915 were extremely vulnerable on the ground. Remember, that in flying trim, an airship is weightless, yet it has a huge side area. Therefore, in anything other than absolute calm, lighter-than-air craft need hundreds of men to 'hold them down'. During the First World War, the Germans used rails and trolleys to take their Zeppelins in and out of their sheds. They even built a double revolving shed. Beyond that they relied upon manpower. Hence, on many occasions Zeppelins were kept in their sheds – even in weather suitable for flying – because of the difficulties involved in taking them out safely.

Britain of course had the same problems. However, by 1920, experienced British airshipmen had devised a method of mooring airships to high masts, enabling them to be moored in all normal winds with the aid of only two dozen men. The later mooring-masts supplied water, fuel and gas to the mast-head which meant that an airship need never be shedded except for major overhaul. The R.33 spent three months at the Pulham mast in 1921 riding out storms of over 60 mph.

One gas-cell was deflated, taken out, replaced and re-inflated at Pulham mast-head. Complete engine changes were made. Sadly, with the loss of R.38 (ZR-2) in 1921, Royal Naval interest in airships ceased and the mooring-mast was not developed. However, with the commercial ships R.100 and R.101, sophisticated high mooring-masts were built at Cardington, Montreal, Ismailia and Karachi. Because of the loss of R.101, only the Montreal mast was ever used, during R.100's visit in 1930. Cardington was in constant operation while R.100 and R.101 were flying but upon the sad demise of the latter in October 1930, never used again. All were subsequently dismantled.

American interest in large rigids got under way with the launch of ZR-1 *Shenandoah* in 1923. By this time ZR-3 *Los Angeles* was being built, and to service these two monsters, the US Navy adopted the British high mooring-mast. They also developed a track-and-trolley method of extracting airships from their sheds. Ground-handling was constantly updated by the US Navy and many ingenious adaptations incorporated. After the incident when ZR-3 *Los Angeles* rose vertical to the Lakehurst high mast on 25 August 1927, the decision was taken to stop using high masts but concentrate upon the newly designed low mast which offered several advantages.

Subsequently, the huge airship base at Lakehurst, New Jersey was ideally situated to service the Zeppelin transatlantic flights of the *Graf Zeppelin* and *Hindenburg* during the 1930s. After losing *Akron* and *Macon* the US Navy persevered with a small fleet of non-rigids for coastal work. This core of experienced airshipmen expanded during the Second World War, peaking with 119 non-rigids operational in March 1944, gradually reducing to 10 in 1961. Two remained in service for a short while and on 31 August 1962 the last flight of a US Navy airship took place. Thus ended forty-seven years of constant operation. This huge fleet of quite sizeable non-rigids was only able to operate so efficiently because of the handling experience which stemmed from the early rigid programme.

The US Navy's Second World War airship was a far cry from the Royal Navy's non-rigid of the First World War although the same principles applied. Several types evolved, the workhorses being K-3 to K-135. Known as the K-ships, they were somewhat modified during the conflict but all had the following characteristics: 250 ft long, with a gas volume of approximately 450,000 cu ft of helium, cruising speed of 60 knots and a still air range of 2,000 nautical miles. Powered by two reliable 425 hp Pratt & Whitney Wasp radial engines, their crews (eight or nine airshipmen) were housed in a completely enclosed

US Navy L-8 in the Second World War. A training airship seen here at Akron, Ohio. Note the Goodyear-Zeppelin 'air-dock', with its famous 'orange-peel' doors in the background. The Goodyear L-class non-rigid was used mainly for training aircrew for the larger K-class. (*Ces Mowthorpe Collection*)

control-car with all-round vision through plexi-glass windows. The L-class, a smaller version, was used for training. Towards the end of hostilities, a larger M-class became operational. Postwar, even larger airships were developed, culminating in the large ZPG-3Ws of the late 1950s. These were over 400 ft long, with gas volumes of 1,516,000 cu ft – still non-rigid – they were larger than the early Zeppelins!

This huge fleet was operated by the US Navy on anti-submarine patrols in both the Pacific and Atlantic theatres. Highly sophisticated in their design, they suffered few of the shortcomings of the old Royal Navy ships. Capable of flying in all normal weather conditions for 15 to 24 hours – often longer – their control-cars possessed a standard of comfort unknown in ordinary aircraft, including rest berths for off-duty crew with full kitchen and washroom facilities. Nevertheless, long hours spent searching the ocean for the enemy, or survivors of stricken vessels, in all conditions, was demanding work.

These US airshipmen became highly professional during their careers and contributed, like their RN forbearers, greatly to victory over the U-boat and mine. Fitted out with advanced electronic gear, including MAD (Magnetic Airborne Detector) and radar, techniques were developed that proved very efficient. Their main task was to keep the U-boat underwater, where its relatively slow speed (even in 1944) prevented it getting into an attacking position. Submarine captains were only too well aware that if located, by any means whatsoever, from an airship, that airship could soon summon a whole flotilla of surface craft, putting the submarine in a very parlous position. Airship captains, however, only had to positively locate a submarine, maintain contact and coordinate the surface fleet. On the rare occasion when a U-boat was found on the surface, the airship attacked immediately with depth charges.

Naturally, with such a large fleet of airships, losses did occur, mostly through training accidents, unsuitable weather or plain bad luck. Airships were rarely involved in direct action with the enemy although defensively/offensively, equipped with several .5" machine-guns. Casualties from enemy action were few, but did occur. K-94 mysteriously burned and was lost off Puerto Rico on the night of 30 October 1943 with all her eight crew members. The cause was listed as 'possible enemy action'. 18 July 1943 found K-74 involved in a duel with a German U-boat which refused to dive. Attacking the U-134 with machine-guns while diving to drop depth-charges, K-74 was met by a barrage of fire from the submarines anti-aircraft weapons and 5-inch deck gun. Mortally crippled, the airship crashed into the sea. Fortunately, the wreckage remained afloat until sighted the next day and all the crew were saved except one who was 'lost to sharks'. At least one further blimp went missing, presumed 'lost through enemy action'.

Operational statistics for 1943 are interesting. 17,500 flights were carried out by US Naval lighter-than-air craft, totalling 180,000 flying hours in the Atlantic/Pacific theatres. The Gulf sea theatre contributed another 48,800 hrs, the Caribbean 11,800 hrs and the Brazilian 4,400 hrs – all this in one operational year. The American airshipman had developed his skills to a fine art, better even than his illustrious predecessors.

But accidents did occur. The night of 8 June 1942 saw the collision between L-1 and G-1 out of Lakehurst. Crashing into the sea off Manasquan Inlet, both were lost, with four officers, three enlisted men and five civilian researchers. July found K-6 breaking away from her mast and being written off. Fortunately, there was no loss of life. A truly *Marie Celeste* situation arose on the 16 August 1942. L-8 departed from her station at Treasure Island, San Francisco. Two hours later she radioed that she was investigating an oil-slick. Moffat Field then lost all communication and declared an emergency. Next morning saw the L-8 drifting over the coast and making a safe landing in the main street of Dale City, a suburb of San Francisco. Held down by passing civilians until help arrived, no crew were on board. Everything was normal: radio, parachutes and life-rafts were all in working order. There was plenty of fuel. A cup of cold coffee and a sandwich with one bite taken out suggested a sudden emergency. Despite extensive searching the crew were never found. All crew were in full flight uniform which meant they were wearing life-jackets. No logical explanation has ever come to light.

1943 started badly: K-64 collided with K-7 in poor visibility off Barnegat Inlet, New Jersey. Nine crewmen were lost even though K-7 struggled back to base.

1944 saw two tragic accidents. Practising circuits at Lakehurst, K-5 failed to clear No. 1 shed, crashing into the upper ledge. The gasbag tore and the car, after first being suspended, suddenly broke free, hitting the ground hard, killing the six officers and four crew. The west coast station Del Mar was the scene of a further accident some time later. K-111 struck Santa Catalina Island in dense fog. Her depth charges and fuel tanks exploded, killing six crew. Two survivors were blown clear.

The ocean is a hard taskmaster. It can claim victims at any time even when extreme vigilance is exercised. During the closing months of the Second World War, sixteen lighter-than-air crew were lost in a number of isolated incidents. Flying low over water in reduced visibility caused a number of airships to fly into the sea for various reasons. In most cases, loss of life and craft ensued.

Altogether during the Second World War the US Navy lost thirty-eight of her airships. Thirty-four more were involved in major accidents. Seventy-seven officers and men were killed and that old bogey of lighter-than-air craft, ground-handling, caused six fatal accidents. Set against this is the remarkable record of never losing a single vessel to submarine attack while an airship was in the escort. Except for one possible exception, the RNAS during the First World War could make exactly the same claim.

CHAPTER TEN

Aftermath of the Second World War

Victory in 1945 brought about huge cuts in arms spending by all the Allies. American airshipmen were demobbed and programmes slashed. Anti-submarine warfare had developed highly sophisticated electronic systems. Suitable for aeroplanes, these systems were vastly more efficient when fitted to airships. Slower (an advantage in ASW), with much greater stability and spacious interiors in the control-cars, they proved invaluable, giving better performance. Consequently, the US Navy decided to continue with its lighter-than-air branch.

Greatly reduced in numbers, American non-rigids still comprised a sizeable fleet. New designs were developed; larger, faster and with greater range. During the 1950s a further development was made. The 2W and 3W class became vital parts of the American early-warning system, carrying huge rotating randomes inside their envelopes. Now the professional airshipman – or lighter-than-air crewman – to give him his modern name, became simply another professional flyer, taking to the air in all weathers and carrying out his duty like any other serviceman.

The Goodyear-built ZPG-3W of 1958 was the largest non-rigid airship ever built: 406 ft long, a gas capacity of 1,500,000 cu ft and powered by two Wright Cyclone 1,275 hp engines, mounted inside the two-deck control-car with fully-feathering reversible pitch propellers. This class, four of which were built at a cost of $54 million, were larger than some 1915–16 wartime Zeppelins. Crews consisted of ten officers and fifteen enlisted men.

March 1957 saw the US Navy with a fleet of forty-four airships. Airshipmen were performing tasks which would have been

US Navy's airborne early warning airships started with the ZPG-2W shown here, *c.* 1956. Larger than the early First World War rigid Zeppelins which raided England in 1915, these high-tech non-rigids were virtual flying radar stations. They carried rotating aerials inside the envelope as well as, in the case of the 2W, on top. (*Ces Mowthorpe Collection*)

impossible in 1939: the larger ships were constantly achieving record-breaking long-distance flights. In May 1954, Cdr Eppes was awarded the American DFC and his crewmen Air Medals for an unrefuelled flight of 8.3 days. This was bettered in 1957 when Cdr Hunt circumnavigated the Atlantic ocean in 11 days. Normal 'operational' flights varied between 40 and 70 hours. It was now apparent that the operational endurance of these airships depended more upon the serviceability of their equipment, rather than the human abilities of their crews.

Endurance was not the airship's only ability. They regularly landed on aircraft carriers, refuelled and replenished from surface vessels. An ingenious method of 'remote refuelling' was devised. Huge plastic bags holding hundreds of gallons of fuel were deposited in the ocean at various positions, by parachute, surface vessel or submarine. Located with the airships equipment, the ship hovered above the bag of fuel, hoisting it aboard by means of a powerful winch (standard equipment). Fuel was transferred to tanks, the plastic container being dropped back into the ocean to be picked up, replenished and used again.

Many shipwrecked mariners were rescued beyond the range of the (then) helicopter. In several cases the shipwrecked crew were too many to take on board so the blimp hovered around the rafts until surface vessels arrived – in the meantime supplying hot food and drink from its galley to the sailors.

During this postwar period, direct entry for airship pilots was abandoned. Aeroplane pilots who volunteering for lighter-than-air experience were taken from US Navy. They undertook a four-month transitional training course and a minimum two-year tour of duty. Later models of US blimps did away with the traditional elevator wheel and rudder wheel which were often manned separately by coxswains or co-pilots. Instead, controls, elevators and rudders were serviced by a 'traditional' control column which could, if need be, utilise a standard automatic pilot system. Normal flight instruments were fitted. Because of the reliability of these modern blimps, free-balloon training stopped in 1957.

1960 marked the beginning of the end for US naval blimps. Cuts in naval estimates closed down most lighter-than-air stations. Shortly afterwards tragedy again struck. ZPG-3W, operational for only three months, was flying off the New Jersey coast. The crew heard a loud crack and the airship began to lose height. Despite instant corrective action, she dived nose-first into the sea so quickly that no radio messages were received by Lakehurst. The crew, all surviving the impact, were hampered by the huge envelope collapsing on top of them. Eventually, only three survivors were picked up by a fishing boat. It was the worst non-rigid airship disaster of all time. The other three 3W airships were grounded pending the inquiry. The Board of Investigation report can be summarised thus: 'Primary cause of the accident was the failure of the envelope. The specific cause for this failure has not been identified.' 'Suggestions are that there was a defective envelope seam, perhaps coupled with inadvertent low envelope pressure.' Changes were instituted. Dacron was used instead of cotton for the envelopes. Automatic low-pressure warning lights were fitted to let the pilot know if envelope presure dropped to a dangerous level.

Spring of 1962 saw the termination order for airships written. By the end of November everything was closing down, the final flight being carried out by ZPG-2 No. 141559 on 31 August. With her crew and a chosen few 'old-timers', she rose and cruised off Toms River, landing at 1536 hrs for the benefit of the media. This was the last naval airship flight after 47 years of continuous operations.

ZPG-2 (No. 141559) – the last naval blimp to fly – was used latterly as 'a flying wind-tunnel'. Ordinary wind-tunnels suffer from 'wall-effect' i.e., fluctuations from the tunnel wall affect calculations. No. 141559 had a strong retractable strut fitted to her control-car. Aerodynamic models of all kinds were attached and the strut lowered some 30 ft below the car. Unique data which could not be obtained by any other method was passed to Princeton University. It was a two-year programme, ending finally in August 1962.

Much has been said about the service role of American airships after the Second World War. Remember, the Goodyear Corporation had built most of the American airships since 1918. They also operated a small private fleet of non-rigids between the wars – these were impressed into the US Navy in 1941. Goodyear designed and built, with full naval assistance, the wartime fleet. Hence after 1945 they resumed operations with six blimps – five L-class and one K-class. Mostly used for advertising their own products, Goodyear were not averse to hiring them out for special occasions. In the 1970s, using computerised electronics, Goodyear built two special airships, one based in Europe, the *Europa*, which had thousands of electric bulbs attached to their envelopes. Keying in suitable messages, any words/graphics could be flown through the skies promoting merchandise. Goodyear also operated a training school for airship pilots. Naturally, their instructors and crews were ex-US Navy.

The Douglas Leigh Sky Advertising Corporation purchased a number of L and K-class ships in 1947, leasing naval sheds across the United States and using the blimps for advertising, utilising large banners affixed to the envelopes. Hollywood and the movie world

Compare this picture of Flt Lt Struthers sitting on the open cockpit edge of his Coastal C.9 during the First World War with the totally enclosed cars of the Second World War US Navy blimps. Yet both wars saw these non-rigids perform excellently, and there is no doubt that they saved many seamen's lives. (*Peter London*)

were regular customers and for several years the DLSA Corporation received a grant from the US Navy which considered them a useful reserve. This was not the first time cinema audiences were entrapped by blimps. Howard Hughes bought one (ex-Navy) especially to advertise his film *The Outlaw*, flying over most American cities before or when the film was being shown.

History shows clearly that American airshipmen of all ranks became the most advanced and experienced airshipmen of all time bringing the latest technology and equipment into use. These later blimps had a standard of advanced technical expertise undreamt of in the Zeppelin era. Vast sheds were situated across the country. Superb self-powered stub mooring masts and mechnical 'mules' did away with the large handling parties of former times. Portable masts, serviced by two motor vehicles and six ground crew became available when required. Reliable motors, radios and ancillary equipment enabled operations to be carried out like clockwork. Experienced crews served in blimps for their entire careers. Even the highly-skilled crews of the Zeppelins never acquired such specialised capabilities.

CHAPTER ELEVEN

Small Civilian Operators

The First World War proved the small airship to be a viable, efficient flying machine. There were also many experienced airshipmen and available sheds. However the aeroplane was the chosen vehicle for travel, despite its many shortcomings, leaving airships on the sidelines. Large rigids of the Zeppelin style were obvious contenders for long-distance work. Small non-rigids appeared to have no place in a peaceful world. We saw in the chapter on American airships the disastrous *Wingfoot Express* operation. Goodyear Tyre and Rubber Company – the principle American airship builder – began operating two ships. These displayed the Goodyear logo on their envelopes and flew around the country as an in-house advertising stunt, with considerable effect. They increased the fleet to three and this has continued up to the present time. But they are unique, being not only airship builders but an international company of such magnitude that they could afford the operation.

Europe, suffering the aftermath of the war was busy expanding its aeroplane culture. However, 1929 saw Capt Weir-MacCall, J.R. Pike and Engineer R.H. Schlotel designing, building and flying the AD-1, a 60,000 cu ft single-engined non-rigid with a two-seat car, to be used as an advertising medium. She was tested for her Certificate of Airworthiness by Capt George Meager – a very experienced First World War airshipman and at that time, First Officer on the R.100 – on 6 November 1929. Previous to this, during her trials, flights had been made over the Newcastle Air Pageant. Capt Beckford-Ball took over from Capt MacCall during the trials when a large banner displaying 'THIS SPACE TO LET' was affixed to the envelope. It was unfortunate that the 75 hp ABC 'Hornet' engine, chosen for economy, left the airship under-powered. Deflated over the winter months, she was re-rigged and flown again in May 1930. Later that summer an ex-RNAS Rolls-Royce 'Hawk' engine was fitted which improved performance.

AD-1 is seen here at her Cramlington base near Newcastle on 13 September 1929. These were her first trials and she did not receive a Certificate of Airworthiness until 6 November 1929. Large linen panels were fastened to her sides and used for advertising purposes. (*Ces Mowthorpe Collection*)

Logos for 'WILSON'S FINE FOODS' and 'GOLD DOLLAR CIGARETTES' were two of the banners displayed. This gallant venture, always under-funded, came to a sad end when AD-1, having flown across the Channel, was wrecked while moored-out, in a storm at Ichteghen on 7 October 1930. The remains were auctioned off on site for a total of £32 10s. It was commendable, and a tribute to their wartime naval training, that Capt Beckford-Ball and his crew operated an airship for six months, on a business basis, without the back-up of a large organisation.

Capt Beckford-Ball was again in the airshipman role in 1951. Lord Ventry, a staunch believer in airships, raised funds to build a small non-rigid of 45,000 cu ft. The envelope was adapted from a redundant French kite balloon and with the help of ex-First World War airshipmen, successful flights were undertaken, purely for sport. Other old-timers were Capt York-Moore, Gerry Long, Freddie Twinn, Ralph Deverall, Arthur Bell, Joe Binks, Alex Leith and A.L. Speed. Partially funded by a grant from Bournemouth council as part of the Festival of Britain, it was named *Bournemouth*, registered G-AMJH and carried a pilot plus three passengers at a speed of 27 mph. An old omnibus had a small mooring-mast attached which provided 'local' mooring-out. Sadly, during the 1953 inflation at Cardington, some netting, stored in the roof of the shed, fell onto the envelope, damaging it beyond repair.

Between 1974 and 1976, two enthusiasts, Anthony Smith and Jasper Tomlinson flew a 30,000-cu ft airship, which they had

Under the late Lord Ventry, a committed lighter-than-air enthusiast, a team of First World War airshipmen, aided by younger members, built this little airship from the envelope of a disused French observation balloon. A grant from the Bournemouth town council assisted – hence the name. Shown here at Cardington, prior to her first trial flight, July 1951. (*Lord Ventry via Ces Mowthorpe Collection*)

designed and built at Cardington. Following initial teething troubles, a number of successful flights were carried out. Registered G-BAWL (unofficially named *Santos-Dumont*) it was finally wrecked when inadvertently flown into some trees after a visit to Old Warden in 1976. Another magnificent lighter-than-air venture ceased to exist.

Roger Munk's beautiful Skyship AD500 and successors, graced Bedfordshire skies during the 1970s and '80s. During 1987, Skyship

Skyship 600, G-SKSC, first flew in March 1984. Seen here moored to her portable mast at Cardington in November 1987 where she, for a short period, took eight passengers for one-hour flights over central London at £100 per head. (*Ces Mowthorpe Collection*)

149

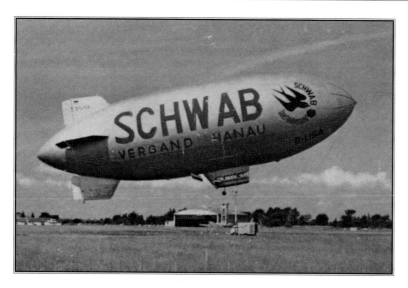

The ex-US Navy L.19, with an enlarged envelope, operating over Germany in 1966. (*Wg Cdr Dunn via Ces Mowthorpe Collection*)

AD600 (G-SKSC) flew from Cardington with up to eight passengers at £100 per head on sightseeing flights across London. Special dispensation by CAA permitted these flights. By the late 1990s, Roger Munk's design appeared to have taken off in other parts of the world. Westinghouse Airship Industries (WAI) developing it as the Sentinel 5000 for the US Navy.

As always, it was financial problems which brought these ventures to a close, not the airshipmen.

Germany, while concentrating upon its giant Zeppelins between the wars, also had the Parseval *Natz*. This large non-rigid was based upon the wartime PL-25 and used as a joyriding and training ship. During the late 1920s and early '30s it was flown regularly. It is always assumed that airshipmen are of the male variety but occasionally women did penetrate into their ranks. During 1930 the *Graf Zeppelin* had a female engineer as a regular crew member. In the same year Frau Sophie Thomas of Berlin qualified as an airship pilot, presumably on the *Natz*. The latter was certainly the only woman to qualify as a airship pilot in the world. Sadly the loss of the *Hindenburg* in 1937 brought to a close all lighter-than-air activities in that country.

German industry, rising out of the ashes of the Second World War, again foresaw the advertising potential of a 'blimp'. A small airship, slowly flying around a city at less than 2,000 ft creates considerable interest. If on the ship's side is a product's brand-name or logo, and the ship is airborne for several hours, it becomes quite a talking point, thus enhancing the product. The American Goodyear blimps are excellent examples. During the mid-1950s, an ex-US Navy L-class, the L-19 was bought by a German company.

L-19 first was fitted with an enlarged envelope (158,000 cu ft) and the brand-name Guldenring emblazoned upon it in 1956. After operating for a few years the logo was changed to Underberg. This remained until 1961 when a further logo change to Schwab took place. Throughout these commercial operations the ship carried the German registration D-LAVO until sold to Japan in 1968.

Alongside the above airship, was the *Trumph* (D-LEDA), built by Ballonfabric-Augsburg in 1956. Unlike the ex-US Naval L-19, *Trumph* was single-engined and smaller. Both these blimps were flown regularly and on at least one occasion, operated together. At this time, the two crews, each consisting of two pilots (Americans) were the only qualified airship pilots in Europe. *Trumph* was damaged in a storm while riding at her mast and dismantled. She was replaced by a larger, twin-engined ship, built by Ballonfabrik und Metallwerk in July 1958. This new *Trumph* was the first ship in Europe to operate with helium and was still flying in the late 1980s.

In the 1950s, Herr Wullenkemper of Westdeutsche Luftwerbung, Mulheim, built an airship similar to the twin-engined *Trumph*. Designated WDL-1, she advertised Wickuler and Der Fliegende Musketier.

All these blimps were to be found flying around Europe, together with the better-known Goodyear Europa during the late 1970s. They operated away from base with portable mooring-masts and a ground crew of four or five, transported from site to site in two motor vehicles. These commercial operations occupied the summer months. During the winter months, the ships were deflated and overhauled in their sheds. Portable mooring masts for non-rigids were pioneered by RNAS airshipmen of the First World War and brought to sophistication by the US Navy by 1939. Collapsible but strong, these masts have moored blimps in gales up to 60 mph on occasions, the airship having a 'watch-aboard' at all times. This can consist of a single ground crew under normal conditions but if weather deteriorates a pilot climbs on and starts the engines. By skilful use of controls the ships can be kept head to wind and stable. The Americans call this technique 'flying the mast'.

One of the chief advantages to come from these small operations is that they have retained a core of highly-skilled airshipmen, familiar with modern practices. Likewise, their constructional designers and staff have ensured that airships retained a place in world aviation. The end of the twentieth century has seen several projects beavering away on a world-wide basis. Roger Munk's AD-600s fly in America and Japan,

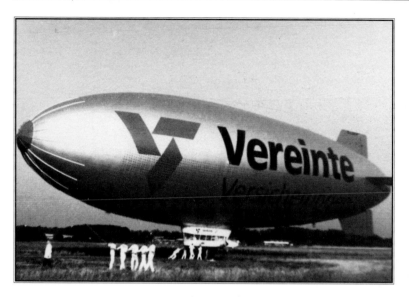

The German advertising/
passenger-carrying WDL, seen
here in 1962, operated
sightseeing flights over Central
Europe. (*Ces Mowthorpe
Collection*)

familiar to millions of television viewers as they float above international
sporting events, providing a stable base for television cameras, the
Japanese firm Fuji being well to the fore. Fuji not only get paid for by
the television company, their logo gets world-wide publicity!

Germany's Zeppelin company has built and flown a large non-
rigid to be used commercially. Designated NT she made her maiden
flight in September 1997 and advertised Stuttgarter Hofbrau.

The combination of electronics and computers allow infinite
variations of lettering and logo on the sides of an airship's envelope,
even a form of 'moving picture'. Impressive by day, these superb
machines, floating in the night sky are positively startling. 1993
revealed another 'bright' venture by airshipmen. The American-
built A-60, operated by Virgin Lightships on the continent, is flown
by an ex-RAF Navigator, Alan Burrows. This small twin-engined
blimp has a capacity of 60,000 cu ft, using helium as the lifting
agent. The interior of the translucent envelope is illuminated by
electricity and glows brightly against a darkened sky – the initial
advertising was for the newspaper *Der Tagesspiegel*, the words
standing out boldly. Her control-car/gondola can carry up to four
passengers.

Thus it appears that after a void of nearly twenty years, following
the *Hindenburg* tragedy and the Second World War, airships have
again found a useful place in Europe's aviation history, largely as a
result of America's war and postwar experience.

The present-day airline passenger will always owe a considerable

The Goodyear *Europa*, in England in 1971, during one of her annual visits before her unfortunate demise. (*Ces Mowthorpe Collection*)

debt to airshipmen. In-flight catering was born and developed in airships. Aviation meteorology, pioneered on a world-wide basis by the RAF and British Civil Aviation for the proposed Empire airship route, which came to a halt with the loss of R.101 at Beauvais on 5 October 1930, is the basic meteorology structure used world-wide today. Radio direction finding, so vital to airliners before the introduction of commercial radar, was being used successfully by the German Zeppelins in 1918. Pressure-pattern flying, used by all international pilots prior to the commercial jet engine, was honed to perfection by Dr Eckener's *Graf Zeppelin* flights of the late 1920s and early 1930s. These and many lesser benefits are a direct result of that band of brothers, now almost extinct, called airshipmen – true sky-sailors.

The A-60 Plus, operated by Virgin Lightships, very small but capable of carrying 3/4 passengers. The A-60's great innovation is that the envelope is lit from the inside – thus at night she is like a flying light-bulb with the advertiser's logo illuminated in glorious colour. (*Ces Mowthorpe Collection*)

CHAPTER TWELVE

Conclusion

The halcyon years of the airship were between 1900 and 1937. As the millenium approaches, fewer and fewer people are aware of these earlier craft. As seen in the last chapter, a small presence is still with us, perhaps even growing. But these modern airships are sophisticated machines made from the latest plastics, with ultra-reliable motors and all the electronic gadgetry currently available. While worthy successors, filling a small niche in the present aeronautical world, they bear little resemblance to their illustrious forebears.

It is the horrific tragedies the public remember, especially that cine-film of the tragic loss of the *Hindenburg* which was flashed across the world's screens within hours of the accident. Even in the late 1990s, any mention of airships on television or in the press is usually preceded by the film or photographs of the *Hindenburg* disaster. Yet, those thirty-six lives lost were the only paying passengers ever killed by Zeppelin airships. Many thousands of others were carried safely as Zeppelins and their crews circumnavigated the world, operating a regular transatlantic service (including South America) during summer months. Wartime apart, airship travel, even using hydrogen as the lifting gas, proved the safest form of mass aerial transportation prior to the Second World War. Altogether the world saw over six hundred practical airships, of all sizes and nationalities, built and flown.

More vital even than these airships were the men who built and flew them. Any serious researcher will keep coming across the same names over and over again. In Germany they were: Count Zeppelin, Dr Eckener, Pruss, Von Schiller, Parseval, Professor Schutte, von Buttlar, Lehman plus a few hundred more.

In Great Britain: Sir Murray Sueter (Admiral RN), Cdr Masterman, Capt (later Air Commodore) Maitland, Cave-Browne-

Cave, Rope, Scott, Usborne, Wg Cdr Cunningham, Sir Barnes Wallis, Struthers, Cook, York-Moore, Long, Hunt, Meager, Beckford-Ball, Williams and too many more for individual mention.

In Italy: Nobile, Colonel Tombesi, Usuelli, Borsalino, Munari, Crocco and the Forlannini company. The Norwegian airship captain, Maj Gen Hjalmer Riiser-Larsen, trained in England by Capt Maitland will forever be associated with the two great Italian airships used by Gen Nobile for his Arctic flights *Norge* and *Italia*.

France can claim General Joux, Count de la Vaulx, and although a Brazilian national, because all his flying was done in France, the redoubtable Santos-Dumont; the Astra and Astra-Torres company; the Zodiac Company, Clement-Bayard and Lebaudy.

America, slow to operate airships, but going on to become the greatest user of lighter-than-air craft that the world has seen, had the following outstanding airshipmen: Capt Maxfield, Admirals Rosendalh and Moffat, Capt Landsdowne, Commanders Dresel and Wiley with many subordinates and crewmen. The American Goodyear company will forever be linked with American lighter-than-air history.

Present-day travellers take for granted that amazing invention of the late Air Cdre Frank Whittle – the jet engine. This power-unit alone enables modern passenger jetliners to cruise safely 'above the weather' and electronic marvels enable those same jetliners, manned by superbly-trained pilots, to land safely in all conceivable weather conditions.

Yet many of the disciplines, training and practices in handling jetliners in all weathers were instigated by airshipmen. Without any of the modern devices, they persevered in operating for long periods, over unseen territory, in uncertain weather conditions, yet still arrived safely at their bases.

Much of the aerodynamic technology applied to the modern airliner originates from the airship designers' work with solid bodies in flight; pitch, roll and yawing, the control of these movements in flight and consequent effects on stability and control. When Great Britain had high hopes of an Empire airship service, the Aeronautical Research Committee studied deeply the problems associated with the three-dimensional flow over elongated bodies. While the horrific tragedies of R.101 and the *Hindenburg* brought about the end of commercial airship development, these studies again become relevant when applied to modern aeroplanes. The development of the large aeroplane piston-engines owed much to the earlier airship engines which had to perform for hours on end, rather than minutes. The late Sir Barnes Wallis produced a paper 'The Application of the Aerodynamic Properties of Three-Dimensional Bodies to the Stabilisation and Control of Aerodynes' which laid down many basic principles for the swept-back and variable-geometry wings in use today.

When the aeroplane flights were recorded in minutes, or at the most two or three hours, airshipmen stayed aloft for days. Aerial navigation, originally based upon the maritime system of deduced reckoning, involving time and distance, became an art of vital importance before the days of radar and electronic/satellite computers. Airshipmen pioneered this art.

Meteorology for the airman was a little-known science (called Aerology prior to the 1920s). However, when Great Britain decided to compete with the German Zeppelins and institute the Empire air routes, using the ill-fated R.101 and sister-ship R.100, meteorology was taken seriously and air masses studied in great depth. The loss of R.101 in 1930 put an end to the Empire airship link. The meteorologists carried on for the up-and-coming Empire air routes, reaching a peak of expertise in the Royal Air Force of the Second World War.

Radio navigation for aircraft was pioneered by the German Telefunken company in 1915, in order that the wartime Zeppelin captains had an alternative to deduced reckoning. Today, radio/electronic navigation is the norm. Certainly it would have developed with the intercontinental airliner, but, when required, it was already available – it had been used first by the airshipmen.

Those early airship days, prior to the First World War, formed the basis upon which world-wide travel for the masses would eventually become the norm.

Perhaps some day, one of the millions of passengers, departing General de Gaulle airport, Paris, will look down on the city and think of Santos-Dumont with his little No. 9 airship, sailing over the rooftops, looking out for his friends in the Champs-Elysées, then dropping down to share a glass of wine, his little airship tied to a convenient adjacent balcony. That occurred ninety years ago – the first practical air traveller.

APPENDIX 1

Airship Sheds

While flying through the skies, airships behave predictably. Safely housed in their sheds, the same applies. It is, however, the transitional stage where the airship is being transferred from her natural element, into the security of her shed, which has taxed the ingenuity of airshipmen.

Because an airship is buoyant, lighter-than-air and very large, the slightest crosswind presents problems. During the early days, airshipmen simply chose to fly when weather conditions were most suitable. This was usually early in the morning or during the evening. Half a dozen men would walk the craft out of its shed into the centre of the airfield, wait until the relatively short flight was over, then re-house the ship.

Naturally if airships were ever to become practical propositions they had to be capable of operating in winds up to 35–40 mph. Controlling them on the ground in these winds was impossible unless the wind was blowing from ahead or astern. Small non-rigids were difficult but housing a huge Zeppelin was almost impossible.

Dr Eckener, Flight Director and pilot of the LZ-8 *Deutschland 11* found this out on 6 May 1911. As related in a previous chapter, he was running passenger flights from the Düsseldorf shed. This large wooden airship shed had been hurriedly built by the city of Düsseldorf, who wished to cash in on the new-fangled airship flights organised by DELAG, ahead of rival cities. This shed was built in an open area and subject to unpredictable, fluctuating winds. To minimise the affect of these winds, DELAG had built large windsceens at either end, 50 metres long. As we saw earlier, that day, Dr Eckener, with a full complement of passengers, found himself and his airship literally wrapped around the shed. Fortunately no one was injured.

Another passenger Zeppelin was by now almost completed, the L.10 *Schwaben*. Dr Eckener moved the DELAG operation to Baden-

Oos where he purposely built the shed in a sheltered valley facing prevailing winds. In addition to windscreens, he installed 'docking-rails' extending through the shed and several hundred metres into the field on either side. On these rails were two trolleys which could be securely fastened to the keel of the Zeppelin, fore and aft. Precautions such as these became the norm for all German airship operations both in war and peace. Operating out of Baden-Oos *Schwaben* was still able to use the Düsseldorf shed – but only when weather conditions were suitable.

The German Navy, conscious of all-weather wartime operations, built two huge double sheds which were revolved by powerful motors, one at Blisdorf, near Berlin and the other at their Nordholz airship base, near the North Sea coast. Capable of housing the largest forseeable Zeppelins, this double shed weighed over 4,000 tons and could be revolved through 360 degrees in an hour. While a practical solution to the Zeppelins' operational needs, this revolving-shed principle was never repeated due to the complexity of manufacture and early teething troubles with the rotational gearing. An unexpected complication was that in freezing wet or snow conditions, the turntables froze solid and the sheds could not be turned. As Zeppelins grew in size, wooden extensions were fitted to both ends. These were nicknamed 'busen', from their similarity to the upper portion of a woman's body.

Important German airship bases, were subsequently built with four or more sheds, double or single, dispersed around the landing-ground. This ensured that at least one Zeppelin was available to fulfil the German Navy's needs, whatever direction the wind was blowing.

During 1915, a new Naval airship base was established at Alhorn, near Bremen, 60 miles from the North Sea. It was fully operational in September 1916, becoming the operational HQ of Fregattenkapitän Peter Strasser, Chief of the Naval Airship Division. Alhorn had four double sheds and it was here, on 5 January 1918, that a remarkable occurrence took place.

Christmas 1917 found Alhorn's Zeppelins weatherbound inside their sheds. Nevertheless regular maintenance and overhauls were taking place, readying the ships for action once the weather broke. Shed 1 was occupied by L.51 and L.47. Shed 2 held L.58, Shed 3, L.46 and Shed 4, the new, huge SL.20, built by Shutte-Lanz, which was undergoing repairs after her trials flight.

Korvettenkapitan Schütze of L58 was walking past the operations room at about 1700 hrs when he saw his chief, Strasser inside. Entering, he engaged Strasser in conversation and the two men were

This picture of the Howden No. 2 Shed was taken in July/August 1921 while R.38 was being repaired after her third flight (from Cardington). At the railway-line junction (bottom left), the line branched off directly into the shed through the door in the centre. A full-size steam locomotive and trucks could be moved between the splayed feet of the centre pillars. (*T. Jamison*)

standing near one of the windows, overlooking the field as dusk was beginning to fall. Both men were horrified to see Shed 1 suddenly burst asunder with a massive explosion. Glancing towards Shed 2, Shütze saw his ship in flames which then gave way to explosions as the gas in L.58 exploded. On the other side of the field, Sheds 3 and 4 were both being blown apart. Within 60 seconds the mighty Alhorn sheds, with their five 'front-line' airships, were reduced to scrap-iron.

Dashing outside, the two officers scanned the sky thinking that an air-raid was in progress. But there were no aircraft, only an eerie silence broken by the crackle of flames from the burning wreckage. After organising assistance for any survivors, Strasser ordered the guard to cordon off the base thus rendering escape impossible for any saboteurs.

When order was again established, the grim cost of this incident became apparent. Ten airshipmen men had died, thirty more were seriously injured with 104 walking-wounded. Four civilian workers also died.

What caused the explosions? This question has never been properly answered. No evidence of sabotage could be unearthed in the remains but that explanation is still uppermost in some airshipmen's minds. In December 1917, the German Navy was beginning to be undermined by propaganda from the Independent Social Democrats, although the airship branch remained steadfast to its officers. At least two German sailors boasted about 'burning Alhorn down' in the postwar period but both were dismissed as drunken braggarts. Indeed, it was proved that one of them had never set foot on the Alhorn airship base. Certainly there is no apparent record of any Allied connection which, had there been, would have become a classic example of successful sabotage and hence eventually come to light in postwar years.

Lt Bassenge, executive officer of L.47 was in his ship when he saw flames, 'in the hull of L.51, over the rear gondola, which was being cleaned by crewmen'. All managed to get outside the doors before the gas exploded.

The Court of Inquiry felt that probably a piece of asbestos from the roof, loosened by the recent bad weather had broken away, crashed through the hull of L.51, breaking some bracing wire which caused a spark and ignited either petrol fumes or escaping hydrogen gas. The Germans always built their airship sheds well apart on the assumption that if one exploded, it would not spread. However the huge explosion of Shed 1, which contained two Zeppelins, L.51 and L.47 – each containing approximately 2,000,000 cu ft of hydrogen, probably sent a pressure wave to Shed 2, causing the gas-cells of L.58 to expand rapidly; and escaping gas from the safety valves became ignited by pieces dislodged from the roof falling through L.58's hull and causing sparks. Similar occurrences caused the blowing up of Sheds 3 and 4.

A further explanation is that contrary to instructions, one of the airshipmen cleaning the rear gondola of L.51 was wearing studded boots instead of the proper authorised rope sandals. It was known that some airshipmen preferred to use petrol for cleaning interiors (against standing orders) rather than the non-inflammable cleaner specified. These two errors, compounded, could have started the initial fire.

Illumination for the men cleaning L.51's car was provided by two electric lights on long leads which entered the car on each side through opened windows. By Christmas 1917, the Allied blockade was really beginning to tell on the German nation. Rubber for insulation purposes had been replaced by ersatz compounds. Lt Bassenge reported that he heard a mild explosion from the direction of L.47's rear gondola through which the leads to the lamps led. He voiced the opinion that faulty insulation on these leads could have caused a short circuit, igniting the petrol fumes which were ever-present in engine-cars. The rear gondola of L.47 contained an engine.

Fregattenkapitan Peter Strasser, already suffering substantial losses to his Zeppelin fleet from the British aeroplanes and their incendiary bullets, is said never to have recovered from this loss to his command. It is greatly to his credit that the Alhorn base was rebuilt and operating again in the last few months of the war.

The building of airship sheds for the huge rigid airships posed a serious logistic problem in wartime for both the Allies and the

Howden No. 2 Shed in spring 1929 during the building of R.100 by Vickers. The splayed feet of the centre pillars between which a full-size steam locomotive and wagons could be taken on the branch line are clearly seen. No. 2 Shed (Howden) was the largest building in the world when completed in 1919. (*Hull Daily Mail*)

Central Powers. Britain, who had far fewer rigid airships than Germany, is reputed to have used 'enough steel in the erection of rigid airship sheds to have built half a dozen cruisers'. During wartime, the Admiralty considered cruisers to be far more useful than airships. However, the argument put forward by the Royal Naval Air Service was that 'cruisers can be sunk, airship sheds (in Britain) will always remain an asset to the war effort'.

The huge double shed at Howden, the largest roofed structure in the world in 1919, was 750 ft long, 300 ft wide and 130 ft high. Bare dimensions can never truly illustrate the vastness of this cavernous building. The two photographs below gives the reader a better indication of size, especially when it is realised that a full-scale steam locomotive and its wagons travelled between the splayed feet of the central upright.

It was only the impetus of the First World War that stimulated the huge expansion of the rigid airship. While in no way decrying the work of Zeppelin-type airships, one has to consider the massive back-up necessary to operate them successfully. Manpower, steel and general support which had to be used for non-operational purposes, could, arguably, have been put to better use.

America proved during the Second World War that the non-rigid airship, correctly operated was successful. However, it was only the rigid airship which was available for fleet operations and strategic bombing in the First World War. Despite their shortcomings, established, consistent operations requiring long-distance and weight-carrying were only possible using Zeppelin-type airships.

APPENDIX 2

Mooring-Out Sites

As mentioned, airships are at their most vulnerable when on the ground. The only really safe place is inside a shed. However, during the very early days (1911–12) at Farnborough, officers of the Air Battalion No. 1 (lighter-than-air) considered that if airships were to be confined to sheds, they would be virtually useless in any foreseeable mobile war. They were, of course, thinking about the small non-rigid airship with which they were familiar – Britain had no operational rigids, of the Zeppelin pattern, until 1917.

Experiments were carried out by Capt Maitland and his chief instructor Lt Waterlow in the use of elementary short mooring-masts, and utilising shelter provided by suitable woods or similar. During the Army exercises of 1913, in which the No. 1 Air Battalion were invited to participate, the three airships 'No. 4', *Delta* and *Eta* were moored out for several weeks, *Delta* and *Eta* in the shelter of trees at Crookham and 'No. 4' in an old chalk pit at Odiham. Also moored out were the complete handling-crews and essential equipment needed to keep the ships flying.

Airshipmen, both ground and aircrews slept in bell-tents and all transport was horse-drawn, motor vehicles not yet being available. *Delta* and *Eta* carried early wireless-sets, thus providing a useful contribution to the exercises.

Towards the end, 'No. 4' developed serious engine trouble which necessitated returning the airship to Farnborough for repairs. No. 1 Battalion's CO, Capt E.M. Maitland and his chief instructor Lt C.M. Waterlow decided upon a bold plan. Rather than dismantle 'No. 4' and return her by rail, they flew over to Odiham in *Eta*, complete with a strong hemp hawser and towed 'No. 4' back by air to Farnborough. Despite numerous problems, this task was safely accomplished on 20 August 1913. This was the only recorded occasion when an airship has towed another airship.

HMA No. 19 (*Delta*) and HMA No. 17 (*Beta*) moored out behind a wood in the 1913 Army manoeuvres, during which a 50-mph gale was successfully ridden out. (*Ces Mowthorpe Collection*)

After hostilities broke out in August 1914, the RNAS, which had taken over all Britain's airships from the Air Battalion No. 1, earlier that year, formed the Dunkirk Squadron of aeroplanes under the redoubtable Cdr Samson, who constantly harried the enemy in every form possible. Here, the No. 3 (Astra-Torres) under the command of Lt Hicks, joined Cdr Samson and made several useful flights over enemy positions until being ordered back to Britain. While at Dunkirk, No. 3 was moored to a small mooring-mast, designed at Farnborough.

This was not the only mooring out of airships in these early days. A similar mast was erected near Dover for *Delta* and an airship camp established under Capt Hetherington. Sadly, *Delta* (Captain: Maj Waterlow) had a serious engine breakdown on her first patrol, was withdrawn, and the camp was closed.

After the war the large rigid R.33 was moored out to a short portable mast, for several days, on the edge of Croydon Airport in late 1920 while checking-out the airports night-flying lighting.

Wartime considerations initially centred upon the larger Royal Naval Air Service 'war-stations' down Britain's east, south and west coastline, at Pulham, Howden, East Fortune, Capel, Polegate, Mullion and Anglesey. These war stations, when they became fully operational, provided every need required for their airships and airshipmen. Capel, Polegate, Mullion and Anglesey were ideal, being right on the coast only a few minutes' flying-time from the sea. Some of the others were less so. Howden, for example, was 30 minutes flying-time from the North Sea. With a head-wind this could easily be doubled. In 1917,

HMA No. 3 moored out to a mobile mast while operating with the RNAS Eastchurch Squadron at Dunkirk, August 1914. (*JMB/GSL Collection*)

when the excellent little 'Zero' airship began to be available in larger numbers – over seventy were eventually built – the idea of mooring-out stations again became a reality. By the time hostilities ceased in November 1918 there were at least sixteen operational mooring-out sites active, with several more in the pipeline.

Mooring-out sites were usually simply a clearing, capable of housing two 'Zeros' with perhaps a third, in an emergency being housed at the entrance, cut into a large plantation of trees situated alongside a large field, suitable for flying. To facilitate maintenance, pits were often dug for the airship cars, thus lowering the envelope almost to ground level where it was then firmly secured to screw pickets which were concreted in. All the airshipmen, air and ground crews lived a carefree life in bell-tents, free from the harsher discipline of 'war-stations'. Hydrogen was stored in pressurised cylinders, and petrol stored in mobile tankers, with a small number of depth bombs tucked away in a far corner of the flying field. Regular deliveries from a nearby 'mother' war-station kept these services topped up.

When major servicing became necessary, or in the case of deflation, airships were flown or sent back to their mother station. Coming as they did late in the war, when the Royal Naval Airship Service had become an extremely sophisticated anti-submarine and anti-mine weapon, mooring-out sites were a very efficient extension of the lighter-than-air branch. Sometimes a major war-station would have two or three mooring-out sites, sometimes up to thirty or more miles away.

The affect of a mooring-out site suddenly thrust upon a quiet country village caused a major disruption to a life-style which had

RNAS mooring-out site in Bochyn Woods near RNAS Mullion, Cornwall, 1917. Note how 'pits' have been dug for the car/gondola of the airship (an SS Zero). The two other Zeros in the entrance do not have any pits. (*Imperial War Museum*)

existed unchanged for many years. After the initial shock however, things settled into a routine which became very beneficial to both country dweller and airshipmen. Firm friendships ensued. Airshipmen lived on a diet of fresh eggs, rabbits, game of all kinds plus of course, home-cured bacon. In return, local landlords and trades-people prospered. So did the local church congregation. Even the village postmistress, although pestered with large bundles of service mail and innumerable telegrams, generally admitted that life was much livelier. Needless to say, many local lasses found themselves husbands.

Compared with the usual naval establishments with their guarded entrance, barbed-wire perimeters and enclosed sheds, the relative freedom of the mooring-site was unique. Apart from a sentry on guard at the entrance, no other form of prohibition existed. Locals, especially young boys, could see everything that went on from behind adjoining hedgerows, and many a countryman, too old for active service, had his mind opened as to what modern total warfare had become.

LZ-127, *The* Graf Zeppelin

If any single aircraft truly deserved the title 'Queen of the skies' it must be the *Graf Zeppelin*. For nine years between 1928 and 1937 she flew the world. She safely carried her crews and hundreds of passengers from the Arctic to the tropics in relative luxury. It is almost impossible to appreciate the magnitude of her achievements today, when thousands of airliners criss-cross the skies above all continents and oceans on regular schedules.

This book is about airshipmen, not airships. However the *Graf* – as she was affectionately known to her crews, was flown by a regular hard core of ex-wartime crewmen whose names were bywords for outstanding professional Zeppelin airshipmen. Therefore, this appendix, showing just some of her adventures, is a tribute to her crewmen and their outstanding Capt, Dr Eckener.

After the highly successful transatlantic flight and subsequent handing-over of the LZ-126 *Los Angeles* to the Americans, Dr Eckener was acutely aware that unless another ship was built in the near future, the whole expertise and capability, possessed by the Zeppelin company, would disperse and be lost forever. Confident that if a suitable airship was built, utilising still available crewmen, it could be made to pay its way and pave the road for future development.

The key was transatlantic travel. Countries were vying with each other to provide the fastest ocean liners to serve the apparently inexhaustable supply of luxury passengers eager to cross the ocean. Airships, even with a ground speed of only 50 knots were twice as quick, thus halving the crossing time. Everything was in place except the money required to build a suitable Zeppelin.

Eckener knew the German people. Even in their drastic financial straits, following their defeat in the war, they might be willing to give the 4,000,000 marks necessary for a new passenger-carrying Zeppelin. As already related, ex-Zeppelin captains and Eckener toured Germany, raising 2,500,000 marks for the Zeppelin-Eckener-Fund. By continuous pressure, Dr Eckener finally got a German government grant for the remainder.

Count Zeppelin, had he lived, would have been ninety on 28 July 1928. On that day, his daughter Countess Hella von Brandenstein-Zeppelin officially christened the LZ-127 *Graf Zeppelin*. Six weeks later, on 18 September, the airship carried out her maiden flight.

After several trial flights the *Graf* rose from her shed and started her first transatlantic crossing. With twenty passengers (only ten were fare-paying) she set course on the 'southerly route' crossing Madeira. South of the Azores the ship encountered a violent thunderstorm. Passing through, she was so severely affected by turbulence that all the crockery etc., on the dining-room tables, which was laid with breakfast at the time, ended up in the passengers' laps, or on the floor. Dr Eckener estimated that these were similar conditions to those which broke up the American *Shenandoah* in mid-air and was delighted that his ship had successfully weathered the storm. However, an urgent message sent him hastily to the port engine-car. Standing on the external ladder he was shown the port elevator from which the bottom fabric was torn and flapping in the slipstream.

Action was imperative. If the fabric was not cut away it might tear further and twist itself around the elevator mechanism, imperilling the ship and all on board. Eckener did not hesitate. Stopping the motors, he asked for volunteers to climb out onto the fin to cut away the offending pieces and secure the remainder. Headed by his son Knud Eckener, the volunteers commenced work, 2,000 ft above the mid-Atlantic. Meanwhile all passengers were assembled in the dining-room and the position explained. With heavy heart Dr Eckener sent out an international 'Mayday' over the radio.

All engines stopped meant the still relatively heavily-loaded *Graf* was slowly losing height and it would soon be imperative to get some forward movement, in order to gain height aerodynamically. Yet Eckener knew full well that the life-saving slipstream over the elevators would almost certainly dislodge the volunteers, led by his own son, from their precarious perches. The airship was 787 ft long and when the altimeter showed 1,000 ft something must be done.

Unable to communicate with the volunteers, Dr Eckener ordered the five motors to be started and run at idling speed, hoping that this would warn the men on the fin and alert them of their position. When the altimeter read 500 ft, it would be imperative to open-up to full throttle, in order to save the ship. Duty-bound to remain in the control-car and unable to see the men outside, including his son, Dr Eckener was in a terrible position. Information fed to him via the crew indicated that his son and compatriots had carried out successful repairs but Eckener could wait no longer. 500 ft was showing and with a swift prayer he ordered full speed. At that moment he received the message that all the volunteers were safely onboard. Ten minutes later, back at 2,000 ft, with the repairs holding firm, the airship continued her flight and the 'Mayday' signal was cancelled. This would not be the only time that Knud Eckener played a prime part in saving his father's airship.

In 1924 the US Army Air Corps made a successful flight around the world – the first aircraft so to do. Dr Eckener was certain that the *Graf* could do the same, more efficiently and carry passengers.

The American newspaper millionaire, Randolph Hearst, put up $100,000 for the American publishing rights, three German firms provided $38,000, paying passengers and stamp frankings on letters carried providing the balance. If successful, this transworld flight would affirm to the world the safety and reliability of Zeppelin airships. One condition laid down by Randolph Hearst was that the flight should 'start and finish with a circle around the Statue of Liberty in New York'.

Passengers sit down at dinner in the saloon of the LZ-127 *Graf Zeppelin*, 2000 ft above the Atlantic Ocean, in 1930. (*Ces Mowthorpe Collection*)

The final route chosen was Friedrichshafen – Lakehurst (New York) – Friedrichshafen – Tokyo – Los Angeles – Lakehurst – Friedrichshafen. More or less, flying at the chosen latitudes, this would trace a 'small' circle course.

With a crew of forty and eighteen paying passengers LZ-127 rose from her base at Friedrichshafen on 1 August 1929. Five days later she landed safely at Lakehurst. Discharging some passengers who were not going on the round-the-world epic, stores were replenished and further passengers, including Lady Drummond Hay (representing the Hearst Press), Sir Hubert Wilkins (the famous explorer) and Cdr Rosendahl (captain of the US Navy's ZR-3 *Los Angeles*).

A successful flight to Friedrichshafen was completed in 55 hours, arriving on the 10 August. Further passengers were welcomed aboard including one Russian, two Japanese reporters and a Spanish doctor. Flying recommenced on the 17 August, overflying Berlin at low altitude and crossing the Russian border at Tilsit. Now the Russian appealed to Dr Eckener to fly over Moscow 'where hundreds of Russians waited to wave appreciation'. Eckener refused, because an anti-cyclone sitting above the Caspian Sea was producing head-winds over Moscow and he wanted to take advantage of westerlies further north. The Russian government representative took this refusal as a national affront and it was only by promising to make a special flight to Moscow, at a later date, that diplomatic relations were sated.

With favourable winds, the *Graf* cruised comfortably at 70 mph on only four engines while beneath, the land gradually became less populated. Rising to only 3,300 ft, the airship passed across the Ural mountains north of the town of Perm. Now, large tracts of unbroken forest containing only large swampy areas abounded. Without any known pinpoints in this vast uncharted land, navigation reverted to the 'dead reckoning' of ocean crossings. The countryside changed to barren tundra over which it is certain (in 1929) no other aircraft had ever flown and was likened by the captain to 'the surface of the moon'. Eventually a huge river was identified as the Irtish and followed to its junction with the river Ob.

Meanwhile, passengers and crew dined in hotel-like comfort, five courses served with the finest wines, before going to their cabins to sleep through the short northern night. Dawn broke as they crossed the River Yenesei, and seeing smoke, an alteration of course brought the airship to a collection of huts, identified as Imbatsk. Course was set from here to the Tanguska river, still crossing nothing but apparent waste and swampland.

This long trans-Asian leg of the flight was made about the 64th N. parallel of latitude. Here, the meridians of longitude are very close. The 'time change' was one hour forward for each seven hours indicated, which bemused the passengers. A deputation approached the captain with a complaint – they were being fed too often!

Passing through a squall without any trouble, a change of course was made the next day when over the river Lena. Flying downriver the airship circled the small town of Yakutsk, dropping a wreath onto the graves of German prisoners of war who died there in the 1914–18 conflict.

Resuming her course, preparations were made by the crew to climb above the Stanovoi mountains which rose to 6,500 ft. The Ayan pass was shown as 5,000 ft and it was over this pass that Dr Eckener guided his ship. Despite rising to over 6,000 ft, the good Doctor estimated they only cleared the top by 150 ft before the ground fell away to the shores of the Sea of Okhotsk. At this point, Dr Eckener worked out that he had more than enough fuel to fly direct to Los Angeles but decided to stick to his flight plan and land in Japan. Altering course, he followed the Japanese islands southwards, touching down at the Tokyo field 101 hs and 49 mins after leaving Friedrichshafen. The *Graf Zeppelin* had averaged 69 mph.

On 23 August the airship departed for Los Angeles. The Russian had left the ship, together with two Japanese reporters, and their places were taken by Lt Cdr Kasuka (A Japanese Naval Aviation Admiral of the Second World War), Maj Shibata from the Japanese Army and another reporter.

The transpacific crossing was completed in record time due to strong following winds but the passengers found it monotonous because most of the flying was in cloud. In the early hours of 25 August, San Francisco appeared upon the horizon, the *Graf* following the coast southwards to Los Angeles. Today, this city's smog problem is well known. It is caused by an inversion (a band of cooler, damper air held firmly down on the surface by an upper layer of warm, dry air) which regularly sits over the city. On the day Dr Eckener approached to land he recorded a temperature of 77 degrees at 2,000 ft, and lower down only 44 degrees. This meant that in the lower, denser air the Zeppelin was 4,000 lb lighter and the only way in which it could touch down was by valving a large amount of hydrogen, which Dr Eckener estimated at 35,000 cu ft. The time taken from leaving Tokyo was 79 hrs 3 mins.

Take-off for Lakehurst was scheduled for the early hours of 27 August. Dr Eckener was unable to replace all the hydrogen valved during landing, and because the inversion over the city was still in place it became necessary to lighten the ship. Surplus fuel and ballast, together with six crew members, who were sent on to Lakehurst by rail, were unloaded. Even so, the Zeppelin would only climb out using aerodynamic lift generated by forward speed. Normally this was no problem but looming 100 ft in the air at the end of the airfield were high-tension cables, supported on pylons surmounted by red warning lights. With a length of 796 ft the *Graf* had no room to spare, and impact with those electric cables meant certain explosive disaster.

Prior to take-off Dr Eckener took his son Knud to one side. He told Knud that he was placing him on the elevator wheel and that he should follow his instructions quickly, without question. Knud agreed and took his place. Passengers said their last farewells to friends, climbing aboard while the engines warmed up. The doors were closed and lines cast off. Standing squarely in the front of the control-car facing ahead, Dr Eckener signalled 'flank speed' on all motors. The *Graf* quickly sped over the ground. Nearing the red warning lights Eckener ordered 'full elevator' to Knud, who spun the wheel immediately. The bows tilted over the high-tension cables and the red lights disappeared below, a violent shudder shook the ship as her bottom fin scraped along the ground. Knud looked questioningly at his father, but the doctor stared straight ahead. Seconds later he ordered 'down elevator' and the wheel was spun accordingly. Slowly the tail of the huge airship lifted over the warning lights and Dr Eckener turned around, patted Knud on the shoulder and relieved him of his post. By prompt disciplined action potential disaster had been averted. That was the second time Knud Eckener played a vital part in saving his father's airship. The bent girders on the bottom fin were repaired at Lakehurst.

Due to her shortfall of lifting hydrogen, the *Graf Zeppelin* flew south, crossing the North American continent at El Paso in New Mexico, thus avoiding the high Rockies and Sierras, before heading northwards for Chicago. Crowds thronged the shores of Lake Michigan as Dr Eckener flew low overhead before setting course for Lakehurst, New York, and a ticker-tape welcome.

The world flight had taken 12 days, 12 hrs and 20 mins. The distance covered was given as 21,250 miles. During the flight an average of twenty passengers had lived in luxurious comfort, eating and sleeping while partaking of an unique flight encompassing lands over which no human had previously flown, and very few even ventured. In 1929 only a German Zeppelin airship could have achieved all this.

The late Wg Cdr 'Wally' Dunn, OBE, who corresponded with the late Knud Eckener, related that Knud recalled his father categorically stating that the *Los Angeles* take-off was the only occasion Dr Eckener felt close to disaster in the *Graf*.

Bibliography & Sources

Primary Sources – Public Record Office

Air. 1.2307	215/19	Air. 1.2398	267/27
Air. 1.2308	215/20	Air. 1.2421	305/18/4
Air. 1.2309	215/21	Air. 1.2654	6/324
Air. 1.2130	207/102/2	Air. 1.2682	204/282/2
Air. 1.2314	222/1	Air. 2.6/1	197/RU.8894, 8895, 9331,
Air. 1.2315	222/6/A		9320, 8892 (174–190) MR
Air. 1.2322	223/41/1265		(5241–55253) (1592–1599)
Air. 1.2397	79022	Air. 2.	173/MR/586 and 1175
Air. 1.2397	267/1, 267/9	Air. 2.	Codes 30–45 (1897–1920)

Published Secondary Sources

Airship Department Admiralty: all classes of Airship Handbooks
Airship Department Admiralty: state of development of Airship Service
Abbot, P., *Airship: The Story of R.34* (Adams & Dart, Bath, 1975)
Abbot, P., *The British Airship at War: 1914–18* (Terence Dalton, 1989)
Althoff, W.F., *Sky Ships* (Orion Books; Crown Publishers Inc., New York, 1990)
Brooks, P.W., *Zeppelin Rigid Airships* (Putnam Aeronautical Books, 1992)
Chamberlain, C., *Airships Cardington* (Terence Dalton, 1984)
Connon, P., *Aeronautical History of the Cumbria, Dumfries & Galloway Region* (St Patrick's Press, Penrith, 1984)
Gamble, C.F.S.,*The Story of a North Sea Air Station*
Higham, R., *The British Rigid Airship, 1908–1931* (G.T. Foulis, 1961)
HMSO, *Various Admiralty Monthly Orders*
Jackson, *Airships*
Kinsey, G., *Pulham Pigs* (Terence Dalton, 1988)
McKinty, A., *The Father of British Airships* (William Kimber, 1972)
Masefield, P., *To Ride the Storm* (William Kimber, 1982)
Meager, G., *My Airship Flights* (William Kimber, 1970)
Raleigh, W. and Jones, A., *The War in the Air* (Hamish Hamilton, Arms and Armour, 1969)
Rimmel, R.L., *Zeppelin* (Conway Maritime Press Ltd, 1984)
Robinson, D., *Giants in the Sky* (G.T. Foulis, London, 1973)
Robinson, D., *The Zeppelin in Combat* (Schiffer Publishing Ltd, Atglen, Pennsylvania, 1994)
Reminiscences, The story of RNAS Polegate
Saville Sneath, R.A., *Aircraft of the United States (Vol. 2)* (Penguin, 1946)
Sinclair, Capt J.A., *Famous Airships of the World* (F. Muller Ltd, London, 1959)
Sinclair, J.A., *Airships in Peace and War*
Toland, J., *Giants in the Sky* (F. Muller Ltd, London, 1957)
Turpin, B., *The Coastal Airship* (Cross & Cockade, 1979)
Turpin, B., *The Sea Scouts* (Cross & Cockade, 1979)
Ventry, Lord and Kolésnik, Eugene M., *Airship Saga* (Blandford Press, Poole, 1982)
Williams, T.B., *Airship Pilot No. 28* (William Kimber, 1974)

A number of sources are also available on the Internet.

Index